About the Author

Steve Johnson was born in Birmingham and has lived most of
his life in Staffordshire. He divided his time through his late
teens and early twenties between art college and running a
caving club. A very varied career has involved working for the
police service, the BBC, self-employment as a graphic designer
and living within the beautiful Cathedral Close in Lichfield
where he works at the Cathedral School looking after the
choristers. He has a lifelong love of music and reading.

Without Favour or Affection,
Malice or Ill-Will

Steve Johnson

Without Favour or Affection, Malice or Ill-Will

Olympia Publishers
London

www.olympiapublishers.com
OLYMPIA PAPERBACK EDITION

A CIP catalogue record for this title is
available from the British Library.

ISBN: 978-1-80439-838-8

This book is memoir. It reflects the author's present recollections of
experiences over time. Some names and characteristics have been
changed, some events have been compressed, and some dialogue
has been recreated.

First Published in 2024

Olympia Publishers
Tallis House
2 Tallis Street
London
EC4Y 0AB

Printed in Great Britain

Dedication

To all my wonderful family and friends.

Acknowledgements

I don't know where to start as there are so many people whom I need to thank for inspiring me to write this and helping me to get to the finished manuscript. Primarily, I must thank John Galilee for all his support, his love, and his guidance and for helping me to move on with my life and my career in a direction I could never have dreamt of. It was John who also suggested that I should write about my police experience.

When I first wrote this manuscript, my long-time friend Gill Davies read through it and we discussed it, and she marked it up for editing. She has also read through the latest updated version of the manuscript and has helped me. Thank you, Gill!

I had lots of support during my dispute with Staffordshire Police, far too many people to list, but the one who stands out and must be mentioned is Richard. Richard had been a police cadet at Rugeley whilst I was stationed there. During my suspension and fight with Staffordshire Police, Richard, by then a young probationary constable in the regular force, openly supported me in front of several very senior officers, an extremely brave thing to do at that time. That support, so openly expressed, meant a lot to me then and always has. It helped me to carry on with the fight. It's officers like that who were needed in Staffordshire Police back then.

My family supported me through such a difficult time, not least my late mother and father, and my two sisters. Everyone in my family was so accepting of my sexuality and whilst John and I were together, he lived much of the time with us, accepted as part of the whole family. What a wonderful family I have.

More recently, as I first revisited this manuscript, right in the middle of the COVID-19 pandemic and lockdown, I must thank all my wonderful colleagues and my friends at Lichfield Cathedral School where I currently work. Not least to Sue Hannam who has given me so much support and, unknowingly, gave me the inspiration to dust down and take a fresh look at my dormant manuscript. Finally, but not least, to Cheryl Baxter for all your support recently.

I really would like to thank all those who looked after me at the station after the assault, when I collapsed, including the ambulance paramedics, the staff at the hospital, most of whom I don't know about when I was unconscious, for all their care.

Foreword

Throughout human history, there are tales that inspire, stories that challenge, and narratives that redefine what it means to triumph against adversity. "Without Fear or Favour, Malice or Ill-Will" by Steven Johnson is just such a narrative - a *tour de force* of tenacity, perseverance, and the unwavering commitment to fighting against the odds. Steve's career in the police force started with great promise until something powerful and troubling stood in the way of his success. His story is not merely a recounting of personal struggles; it is a testament to the resilience of the human spirit and the power of one individual's resolve to combat injustice and facilitate meaningful change. Throughout the pages of this remarkable book, we bear witness to the profound impact of Johnson's experiences - a ripple effect that ultimately resonates positively to the present day. His journey from victim of violence and discrimination to advocate for change, serves as a beacon of hope for all those who have suffered discrimination and prejudice based on homophobia and sexuality.

"Without Fear or Favour, Malice or Ill-Will" is more than a memoir; it is a redemption story for modern times. It illuminates the path from darkness to light, from despair to triumph, and from oppression to liberation. Steve's unwavering commitment to justice and equality serves as a clarion call to all who aspire to create a more just and equitable society.

From the harrowing aftermath of a physical assault to the

steps of Number 10, Johnson's narrative takes us on a journey through recent decades, showcasing just how far one individual, armed with nothing more than an ardent belief in justice, can be the catalyst for change. His story serves as a reminder that even in the face of seemingly insurmountable challenges, hope prevails, and justice can be served.

As you embark on this journey through the pages of "Without Fear or Favour, Malice or Ill-Will," prepare to be shocked, inspired and moved. In the story of Steve Johnson, we find not just a tale of personal triumph, but a blueprint for a more compassionate and just world - a world where the shadows are illuminated by the light of truth and justice, and where the courage of one individual can change the course of history.

Sue Hannam, MA, PGCE, PGLegalDip, LPC, FRSA
Head of Lichfield Cathedral School

Preface

In 2006 under their then Chief Constable John Giffard, Staffordshire Police came out top of the Stonewall Workplace Equality Index of the most gay-friendly employers. It was a noteworthy achievement and there was a lot of news coverage. For a police force to receive that accolade was certainly newsworthy!

It was a remarkable achievement too. Just over a decade before that, I had been battling with Staffordshire Police, as a serving special constable in the force, because I was gay. Homophobia was institutionalised, baked hard into the force right from the top under their then Chief Constable. It is to the credit of John Giffard, who took over as Chief Constable in 1996, that he pushed the force so far away from that hard-baked homophobia. I believe I fired the starting gun which started that journey.

Society has moved on from that period. Being gay in Britain in the twenty first Century isn't the same as it was back in the early 1990s when entrenched homophobic views were still widely held by a significant portion of the (mainly) older generation.

I have changed the names of some of the people who were involved in the events as recounted in the narrative.

Steve Johnson
December 2022

Chapter 1

The Starting Gun

Early Evening. A wide suburban street in a suburb of Stoke on Trent, with terraced houses on either side. No garden and the front doors open straight onto the pavement. Several cars are parked outside houses and lights are coming on as dusk draws on. Families are getting on with their ordinary everyday lives, sitting down for tea or watching TV. Ahead is a wide junction with a road coming in sharply from the left, another road ahead veering slightly left, one diagonally opposite on the right and another road hard on the right. Terraced housing surrounds the wide junction in all directions. All was quiet.

The suburban quiet was interrupted by a small blue car being driven very slowly, hesitatingly, up the road towards the junction, the driver obviously didn't know the location. It slowed as it approached the junction but then pulled over on the left and was parked in a free space. Nothing happened for a couple of minutes. All was quiet again.

I sat surveying the scene, shaking and extremely nervous. Finally, I reached down and turned off the car engine. Looking at my A2Z maps of this part of Stoke on Trent I could see I was two streets, a couple of hundred yards, from the road I wanted. I looked nervously at my watch. Still, a few minutes to go; I was early. I looked around. Lights were coming on in most of the houses. Who knew what stories and what issues were going on in any of those homes? What battles were they fighting? I didn't know it then but a major, life-changing series of events were going to erupt in my life in the not-too-distant future. What was about to happen, had I known it, was firing the starting gun.

Finally, pulling the ignition key out I opened the door and got out. Locking the car door, I set off hesitantly up the road. I had memorised where I needed to be and a minute later, I came out on a busier main road. Somewhere up there should be a bookshop. I easily found and walked past the bookshop after a short distance, with relief but also with apprehension, turned around and walked slowly down towards the junction again. I could still forget this and drive back home. I hesitated. This all felt so wrong! Was I being watched? I walked back down the road towards my car. I felt cheap, almost dirty and I also felt extremely vulnerable, but I wasn't going to turn back. I turned around again and walked back up the road.

There was a youngish man in a long, dark coat walking towards me, he fitted Simon's description, and he was looking straight at me. I hesitated as we approached, Simon smiled and introduced himself. After our first greetings I followed Simon into a side entrance next to the bookshop, then up a steep flight of stairs and into a small, cold, and uninvitingly bare office at the top of the building where I was introduced to two other people; I smiled nervously and shook hands. More people arrived soon after. I sat on a chair in the corner, not knowing what to say. The room had a musty, damp smell.

I felt awkward, I didn't know what to do or to say, but they were doing their best to make me feel at ease. They chatted amongst themselves and a lot of what they talked about went straight over my head, it was a completely alien world to me. But at least they seemed like perfectly normal people. This was the first time I had ever knowingly talked to gay people, and what's more, people who knew I was gay too. I was at the office for the Stoke gay helpline. I was invited out for a drink with them at a pub nearby after the meeting and agreed to go along.

Simon pulled up a chair next to me, there was something he had to tell me, he looked serious.

"Steve, I know you've not had much experience of meeting other gay people before, and there are a few things which you ought to know. Listen to what I've got to say, it's particularly important, OK?"

I nodded, eager to hear what he was going to warn me about. He had a small, laminated card in his hand, blue with pink writing on it. Not particularly good graphic design, I thought.

"I've got a card here which has got some information on about what to say if you are ever stopped by the police or arrested for anything. Say nothing to them, do not trust them. You won't get any fair treatment from them if you tell them that you are gay, you may even get beaten up. If you ever do have any contact with the police and need help or advice, there are some phone numbers of solicitors you can contact on the back of the card. Just be incredibly careful with the police, they do not like gay people like you and me, around here; they can be bastards."

He passed me the laminated card. The police, I suddenly realised with a thrill of dread, were the enemy. I was confused; what did this make Simon and his friends? I had not considered it before, but I almost felt that what I was doing now was illegal and it suddenly scared me. I could not help seeing Simon and his friends as the enemy. What were they like? Certainly, very anti-establishment, and very anti-police.

My police warrant card was burning a hole in my jacket pocket. I was terrified of them finding out that I had just joined the police service. I dare not say anything, what would they say or do if they knew? It shocked me, I had not even thought about it before, but I did know that I could never tell any of my new colleagues in Staffordshire Police that I was gay. Apart from Toby, of course. Suddenly I did not feel safe; I did not fit in. I found myself at the centre of a potential conflict in my life and I retreated from it very rapidly.

I had to get away as soon as possible. After the meeting, I was invited to a gay-friendly pub a short distance away, but I felt extremely vulnerable, frightened even; I had to escape. I made my excuse; said I would see them next week and hastily left them as they headed to the pub. Panicking, I walked the wrong way down the street, could not find the car and spent a fraught five-minute walking up and down side streets before I found my car, to my enormous relief. Sitting safely in my car again, I calmed myself down and tried to make sense of my conflicting thoughts. If that was what gay people were like, I did not fit in. How could I ever resolve the seemingly unbridgeable gap between my being gay and my position now as a police officer? Certainly, from the experience I'd just had, I did not fit into the gay world that I had just seen. Forget that! I would concentrate on my police career for now at least. The other problem could wait, I would have to find some other way out of the predicament, another way of meeting gay people. But for now, it was not important. I turned the car around and set off towards home. No way would I return.

Chapter 2

Issues Start to Surface

For most of my life, I lived in Rugeley, a small, Midland market town with a mainly working-class population of between thirty and forty thousand. It is tucked into a hollow in the Trent valley and surrounded to the south by large tracts of pine forest and elevated heathland – Cannock Chase; a natural barrier, thankfully separating Rugeley from the sprawling West Midlands conurbation to the South. This is the town in which I grew up and where I first realised, at about the age of twelve or thirteen, that in some ways I was not like the other lads at school. That I *liked* some of the other lads at school, a lot. Something I could *never* talk to *anyone* about, I could barely admit it to myself. I was gay.

I busied myself with my studies at school, and I became interested in caving at about the age of seventeen, just before going to college to study graphic design. I spent the next few years devoting all my free time, and my not-so-free time, to gaining lots of caving experience with a lifelong friend. We set up a club which grew to about thirty members and we went on to discover a significant amount of previously undiscovered caves in the Staffordshire Peak District. I channelled all my energy into the caving group, organising and leading caving trips and all this time I kept my sexuality to myself.

It was a few years later, during the 1980s, that I became increasingly frustrated with my career as a graphic designer. I became depressed. Somehow, I didn't seem to fit in. Most of my peers were getting on with their lives but I was stuck at home, with my parents. I felt 'different' but couldn't understand why. I had furious outbursts which frightened and upset my parents, but I wasn't angry with anyone in particular. Several times my exasperated parents said there was something wrong with me and I needed to be in a hospital. None of us really understood what was going on and it traumatised all of us. Only much later in life did I discover my 'superpower' and realise how much it has mostly helped me, even if on one specific occasion later, worked against me. But at that time no one had any idea. I really needed to find another path to take, another career.

One evening, after a chat whilst visiting my friends Phil and Gill, discussing where my strengths were, a suggestion they gave me took me completely by surprise. They thought that the police service might be a good career, but it just seemed ridiculous, absurd even. I had never imagined myself in a police uniform. It was not me! Or was it? Toby was a police officer now. I left Phil and Gill's later that evening and set off to walk home with my mind going repeatedly over this absurd suggestion. Trying to imagine myself as a police officer. And suddenly I could. My pulse was racing.

I had known Toby for several years; he had effectively grown up in our caving group. I supervised him when he decided on cave leadership for his interest whilst working for his Duke of Edinburgh Award. He had been the very first person I had ever confided in about my sexuality, the most difficult issue I have ever had to face telling someone. A few months later Toby joined the police service and I had always admired him for it. I had known him throughout his police career, it had been staring me in the face all these years.

In an instant, as I walked home from Phil and Gill's house, I *knew* what I wanted to do. It was a ridiculous notion, I tried to convince myself. But by the time I had reached home, I still had not been able to shake off the conviction. I went to bed that night with my mind in a state of turmoil. I was certain that by the morning, I would be just as frustrated and have no idea what I wanted to do. But that isn't what happened.

I woke up the following morning even more sure that a career in the police was right for me. The fact that this might not be compatible with me being gay hardly entered my thoughts. If it did at all, it didn't appear to be a problem because Toby, who was now a police constable, had been a close friend for several years, who was understanding of my sexuality. I discussed the suggestion with my parents and they too thought it would be a good career choice for me.

One day soon after, my mother pointed out an article in the local paper where the local police inspector was asking for people to apply to join the special constabulary, the voluntary police service. I decided I would apply to join and if, after a few months, it worked out, I could apply to the regular force. I walked down to the police station in Rugeley for an application form and details. I walked home clutching an application form and a glossy booklet selling the special constabulary to me, but I did not need much convincing. I quickly filled in the form and returned it to the station later the same day. Then I waited, certain that I would be turned down. I waited and waited soon realising that joining the special constabulary was just as complicated and took just as long as joining the regulars. But at least I could get on with my life feeling a bit more positive about where I was going.

Eventually, in early 1987, I received a letter inviting me to go to headquarters in Stafford to sit the standard police entrance exam. I had made it past the first stage! On the appointed evening I presented myself nervously at headquarters and was shown to a room upstairs where many other people were about to sit the exam. A couple of hours later after sitting the exam, I chatted with one of the other candidates, Steve Smith who was also from Rugeley. He was a decent, down-to-earth person who was a self-employed car mechanic with a garage in Rugeley. We got on well and wished each other the best of luck before leaving, each as eager as the other to know our results. Steve would not pass the exam this time, but I would see him again soon.

The following month dragged on as I waited for the inevitable rejection letter or phone call. Eventually, I had a phone call from the liaison sergeant at the divisional headquarters at Cannock, I had passed the exam! He made an appointment to come over and see me at home for an informal interview. A week later, the interview was done, and I was waiting again, although slightly more confident now.

Yet more weeks passed, and I was invited to an interview at Rugeley police station where I had a casual and amicable discussion with the officer in charge of it, Inspector Nigel Cooper. He pointed out that upon joining the police service I could lose a lot of my friends, but I had already considered this and told him I was aware that this might happen. As far as I was concerned, if my friends did not like me simply because I had joined the police service, they were not real friends. I was encouraged when, upon leaving, we shook hands and he said he looked forward to seeing me very soon.

A few weeks later I received a phone call from the liaison sergeant at Cannock asking me to meet him at Cannock police station the following Monday morning – to be sworn in and measured for my uniform. To my utter amazement, I had made it! My campaign to change my career had begun.

In the witness box at Cannock Magistrates Court the following Monday, with a bible in one hand, which I was having difficulty holding still, I read out the oath on a card in as clear and firm a voice as I could muster in my nervous state.

'I Steven Paul Johnson of Staffordshire Police do solemnly and sincerely declare and affirm that I will well and truly serve our Sovereign Lady, the Queen, in the office of Constable, without favour or affection, malice or ill-will, and that I will, to the best of my power, cause the peace to be kept and preserved, and prevent all offences against the Persons and Properties of Her Majesty's subjects; and that while I continue to hold the said office I will, to the best of my skill and knowledge, discharge all the duties thereof faithfully, according to law.'

I took a deep breath and replaced the card and bible. I glanced up at the magistrates who smiled back at me, before, very relieved, I stepped back down out of the witness box.

I was now sworn in as a serving police officer. The significance of the oath I had just agreed in court to keep, never left me. I understood it, and still understand it to mean, that everyone and anyone I deal with in my duties as a police officer will be treated fairly and equally and with the same respect.

We were taken to headquarters where photographs were taken, warrant cards issued, and we were measured up for our uniforms in the stores. Training began at the divisional headquarters in Cannock and over the next few months we were all learning criminal law and about police powers, PACE, first aid, drugs and much more. I found that learning criminal law was quite easy for me, it was mostly very logical; black and white. A law was either broken or it wasn't.

Eventually, I received my uniform and a date to start my police duties. Trying on the uniform at home I looked at myself in the mirror and it was strange. The person staring back at me was a police officer; the person staring at the reflection was not. However much I tried to convince myself that I was now a police officer, I was not yet. Suddenly, the thought that I would be patrolling the streets as a police officer was quite frightening. Nevertheless, I phoned my section officer and arranged my first duty for the following Monday. I changed into my uniform, put my tunic, cap, and truncheon into a holdall, slipped on a civilian jacket, and set off on foot, self-consciously, towards the police station. I was excited and at the same time extremely nervous. I was proud to be wearing the uniform, yet also fearful of anyone noticing me.

Rugeley police station is a small, sub-divisional station. Built around the turn of the twentieth Century, it is a solid and re-assuring building set square at the end of Anson Street, standing imposingly looking down the street into the pedestrianised town centre. It has a lot of character, a maze of corridors and stairways and small offices, yet not too big. The walls are thick and solid, leaving the interior cool in summer but keeping it warm during the winter. I had walked past it often but had only ever ventured inside it in the recent past for my interviews. Now I was going down to work from it as a police officer, something I could never have imagined in my wildest dreams a year earlier.

Ten minutes later I was entering the station by the front door. By this time, I already knew some of the officers from the station because of the work I had done over the past few weeks with a summer activity scheme for children run by Staffordshire Police.

Section Officer George Graham met me and took me on an introductory tour around the station, which left me slightly confused about the layout of the interior – George explained that the station originally had living quarters for the officer in charge and his family, hence why there were two landings and two stairways – very confusing for a while. Eventually, I found myself back in the control room at the front of the station. I was quite nervous now; it was time to go out on my first-ever patrol with SO Graham. After signing for my radio and a quick explanation of how to use it and the call signs used by the police – which seemed utterly baffling – we were ready to set off on foot patrol around the town centre.

I put my tunic on, adjusted my cap and followed George out of the safety of the station into the street, feeling extremely self-conscious. Wearing a uniform was not natural. George stopped me in the foyer of the station and showed me how to wear a cap correctly – not like a car park attendant! He adjusted my cap. It was very reassuring now that for the first year of my service, I would patrol in the company of an experienced officer. In a few months, as I gained a lot of experience, it would become extremely frustrating and I would long for the day when I could patrol on my own, fully-fledged. But for the moment I was extremely glad of SO Graham's company, and I kept close by him and left him to do all the talking when members of the public came up to us expecting quick, decisive help, advice, or action.

My career in the police had begun. Only a few months earlier I could never have imagined myself where I was now. In a few months or a year or so, if everything went well, I would apply to and join the regular force.

Over the following few weeks, I performed regular duties, learning the skills of policing very quickly. One evening I found myself in the middle of a volatile situation when gangs of drunken youths, staggering out of the pubs at closing time, gathered as they often did, along Horsefair, the main street through the town lined with chip shops and takeaways which were where everyone headed. Tempers flared and fights would break out spontaneously. Inevitably, as soon as the police turned up to sort it all out, they would all unite by turning their aggression on 'the pigs' which is exactly what happened on this occasion. It was my first genuine experience of aggression at close quarters.

Even though several officers arrived to help, and patrols were turning up from neighbouring towns, we were still outnumbered. The inspector ordered us to remain calm and not to make any arrests unless unavoidable. It was obvious, even to a novice like me that the moment the first drunken youth was arrested, the situation would explode like a well-agitated bottle of pop, and we would be in a mess. For the first time, I experienced real aggression, hatred so thick I could almost reach out and touch and smell it. I remained impassive – professional, I kept reminding myself, as youth after youth, reeking of alcohol, goaded me, face to face. Spitting at me, making threats to me, my wife, and my kids (If only they knew!). Despite being a potentially very frightening experience, I found that I had no emotion at all. Whilst appreciating the danger of the situation, I felt neither fear nor anger. Just blank. It was easy!

The situation eventually calmed down as it slowly dawned on their alcohol-soaked brains that they were getting nowhere. The ringleaders were in time separated, spoken to, and sent on their way home. The crowd slowly disbanded, leaving us standing awkwardly in groups of our own, but highly relieved.

I was back on duty again within a day or two. I got to know

the other officers at the station and was beginning to feel very much at home there. Coincidentally, my friend Toby had recently been transferred to the station, so I already had one long-time friend there soon after I started. My training sessions continued at Cannock police station where I made several more friends from around the division. John had joined at about the same time that I had, although he was stationed at Wombourne, many miles from Rugeley at the southernmost end of the county. We always had a drink together in the police bar after training sessions and quickly became good friends.

I soon found that I enjoyed working with shift two at Rugeley, I got on well with all the officers on that shift, so I began to arrange my subsequent duties to coincide with theirs. Very soon there was even more of a reason for my loyalty to shift two. Dave was transferred to my adopted shift from Cannock, and Dave and I soon realised we enjoyed working with each other. He was in his early twenties, came originally from Stoke on Trent, and had a loud, outgoing, and cheeky personality – quickly becoming the shift if not the station clown. We worked well together and got on brilliantly. Sgt Lakin, the shift sergeant, recognised this and often paired us up on patrol. I learned a lot about policing from Dave. I really liked Dave, which was extremely frustrating as Dave was sex mad – but completely heterosexual and had a gorgeous wife. There was no way that I could ever tell him that I was gay. We became good mates.

I would gladly enjoy hours of patrolling with Dave, even putting up with the frustration of him talking about sex so regularly. Very regularly in fact. He was married but it didn't stop him from picking up girlfriends, and he always told me about his exploits afterwards. I joined in with his banter as best I could, frustrated that I could not be more honest with him, but I dare not.

His exploits became ever riskier, and I did warn him about it. My frustration was expressed more soon after when I had to point out to him that the girl who waited outside the backyard of the station in her dad's Volkswagen Beetle and who followed us around on patrol from job to job was making it all slightly too obvious, and it was *not on!* Dave earnestly agreed with me and a mile up the road pulled up in a lay-by, the Beetle pulled up behind. Dave got out, saying he was going to tell her to stop following us around on patrol. I sat and waited. And waited. Half an hour later he returned, tidying his hair, clipping his tie back into place and with a sheepish grin.

One afternoon a few months later Sergeant Lakin called me into his office as I was getting ready for parade.

"Go and sort Dave out Steve, he needs a shoulder to cry on. I don't know what's the matter but I'm sure he'll tell you."

I found Dave in the mess room on his own, sitting with his head in his hands looking forlorn.

"What's up, Dave?"

"Oh Steve!" he moaned, "I've been a stupid fool, I know you've been telling me so for ages!"

I pulled a chair up next to him and sat down.

"Why, what's happened?"

"After we went out for a drink last night, I went to meet you-know-who for a chat. We drove up into the Chase, somewhere quiet and you know, had a long chat…"

"Yes, I do understand…" I replied, knowing all too well what a long chat meant.

"Anyway, when I came to leave, my car battery was flat…"

"I bet it was!"

"…anyway, I had to get home somehow, so I left her in my

28

car while I drove back to Rugeley in hers. I had to wake Steve Smith up by throwing pebbles at his bedroom window. He came out and got my car started, I got home at three this morning."

"Serves you right, you fool!"

"But that's not all."

"Not all? I should think that was bad enough!" I retorted.

"But then when I got up this morning guess whose Beetle was driving up and down the road outside the house? The stupid idiot must have found my address on something while I left her in my car! I had to go out and tell her to sod off, but Carolyn saw us and realised what was going on. We had a massive row; the local police were called and now Carolyn's gone back to her mother! I swear, Steven I'll listen to you every time in the future!"

"You stupid prat."

I put a reassuring hand on his shoulder.

"Come on, let us go down to the parade room, we'll talk later. You really are a bloody idiot!"

Dave was so frustrating! He was a good mate, and I learned a lot from him about policing. I wonder how he would have taken to me had he known I was gay? I guessed it wouldn't have bothered him now I knew him.

I was enjoying my police duties, I had settled into the routine, was learning the job extremely fast and was beginning to feel like a police officer. That is, until one evening in early October when events took a turn for the worse.

One evening I set off on foot patrol with Rob, one of the experienced special constables who I had not yet worked with. We left the station, and I was about to cross the road into the town centre when Rob stopped me. He pointed to a car parked outside the post office on the opposite side of the road.

29

"Steve, can you tell me why that car isn't displaying a valid tax disc – and why I'm not going to do anything about it?"

I looked over at the car; I knew the answer straight away. My friend Colin was in the army, a member of the Royal Signals; he and his wife Sharon had been exceptionally good friends of mine for several years. They had lived in Germany for a year or so where Colin was stationed. Colin had a special disc in place of the tax disc on his car.

"It's owned by a serving member of the armed forces who is probably stationed in Germany," I replied, feeling smug. This car had a similar disc.

I quickly discovered that my answer was a mistake, although it was correct. Rob, I soon realised, liked to display his authority and superiority. The rest of that duty was strained, and it was awkward to make conversation. I did not enjoy it. I learned nothing about policing and a lot about Rob, and I was glad to see the station again a couple of hours later.

The following day I was back on duty with shift two and Sgt Lakin put me out on patrol with Dave again, things were back to normal.

Over the following few weeks, I performed many more duties, building up my experience dealing with all types of incidents. I was much more relaxed now around the station and felt quite at home there. I talked about my caving experiences and told stories of the caves we had discovered over the years. Toby featured in quite a lot of it; he had been actively involved in the caving group for many years. Then one afternoon in early November, I was paired up with Toby.

There was an awkward atmosphere between us as we left the station. I presumed this to be because of our previously close friendship – now we were together in completely different circumstances. We checked the patrol car before Toby drove out of the station yard and we set off on patrol. I tried to make conversation, but it was strained. Then Toby broke the ice.

"I hear you've been talking about me to other officers around the station," he said, completely unexpectedly. I was lost for a reply, what was he getting at?

"I don't understand what you mean," I answered eventually.

"You know – you've been talking to other officers about what we've done in the past." His voice was cold and hard.

"But I've never said anything against you!" I retorted, "I've only ever mentioned you when I've talked about caving; you were a big part of the caving group, think of all the caving we did together!"

"Just never mention me ever again in the station, is that clear?"

My anger boiled over.

"OK! You never existed. I thought we were friends! I will never mention you again! I just cannot see what your problem is!"

We continued our patrol in silence for a while. I was angry, surprised, and confused. Toby was ashamed to have been associated with me. Eventually, we began to talk again, although very awkwardly. Toby asked me how I was getting on. Despite our earlier argument, we were still long-time friends, I felt. I had been performing regular duties for several months now and had built up experience in dealing with many types of incidents, and I knew everyone at the station. We chatted about my duties and the other officers. I was getting on very well with everyone, although I did voice my concerns about Rob. Toby seemed surprised. He said Rob was a good friend of his, he did not see him the way I did.

We continued our patrol until we went in for our refreshments at teatime. The experience of working with Toby had unsettled me, I had not expected his response. After tea, I went out on foot patrol with one of the specials. I left the station for home later in the day still troubled by Toby's reaction.

I put the incident behind me and continued turning up for duty, increasingly with the shift I got on well with and had adopted. A few days after the incident I had forgotten all about it. I walked back into the station late one afternoon after duty with shift two, ready to go home. Rob passed me in the corridor, he had turned up for duty just as I was leaving.

"Ah, Steve, just the person! Can I have a quick word with you please?"

He gestured for me to follow and led the way into the drying room, where I was heading myself, to hang up my jacket and change to go home. The door shut behind us.

"What do you want?" I asked, puzzled.

"Just to let you know, I've heard that you don't enjoy working with me, Steven, that's all." He smiled, pushed past me in the narrow room and walked out, the door slamming behind him.

I was left on my own, shocked, stunned. My mind was working overtime. The only person who could have told him was Toby, I had told nobody else at all. I had spoken to Toby in confidence as a friend and he had betrayed my trust. Suddenly I felt very vulnerable, I did not feel comfortable at the station. It was not working out well at all. I was visibly shaken and upset, and it took another minute or two before I composed myself and left the locker room. I left the station quickly, eager not to be seen. I briefly considered resigning.

Chapter 3

Learning the Job

It was now quite clear to me that Toby had not wanted me to join the specials at all, he was extremely uncomfortable with my presence at the station. I spoke to my friends Sharon and Colin about it and was further shocked to learn that Toby had been saying uncomplimentary things about me to them.

What was his problem? I realised that the only possible thing he could be worried about was his knowledge of my sexuality. If so, he was being very immature. Would they infer things about him just because we were, or had been, friends? Besides, there was no way that anyone at the station was going to find out about my sexuality, I had no intention of telling anyone there.

At least I had learned one thing. I now knew just what sort of friend Toby had been, I had not really lost anything at all. I decided to put it behind me. Toby did not like me being at the station, so I would not give him the satisfaction of my resignation. And as far as Rob was concerned, so what? Now he knew I did not like working with him, what was the problem with that? I had only expressed an opinion, to which I was entitled. A couple of days later I was walking back down to the station ready to parade for duty with shift two again.

I decided to tell Dave what had happened, and he didn't like Toby either. I was surprised to learn that Toby was not much liked by many of the officers at the station. This knowledge at least restored my flagging self-confidence, and I felt, strangely, because of this incident, much closer to my adopted shift, and much more a part of the team.

I devoted more of my time to police duties whilst continuing my training at Cannock, learning police practice and criminal law. I was determined to do well. I was very unsure even by the time I had started, how well I would do. I had been performing active duties for several months now and so far, everything seemed fine. Policing suited me. I enjoyed the team spirit and the fact that whenever I went on duty, I could never predict just what I might end up being involved with by the end of the duty. And I enjoyed meeting people, lots of people, from every social background.

As my confidence increased and as my colleagues got to know me better, I was accepted even more as part of the team. I was not there, but I was getting close. Then one duty towards the end of March 1989, I made my mark.

I was on mobile patrol with Dave, we were good mates now and I was enjoying the afternoon. We were sent to a reported burglary at a house on one of the estates. This was quite routine for me now; I knew the procedure. Yet, on arrival, it was not as straightforward as we had both expected.

The late-middle-aged couple who greeted us at the door had been burgled; their electricity metre had been broken into whilst they had been out shopping. They showed us the metre and it was plain to see that it had been forced open and was empty. But, we all agreed, there was no sign that anyone had forced entry into the house, and we were assured that the house had been left secure and locked whilst they had been out shopping. The couple seemed genuine enough. Dave asked if anyone else had access to the house while they were out. They had a teenage son, Mark

34

who lived at home, he had been in when they had gone out shopping, but he was not around now.

Dave looked at me and half-smiled. I knew what he was thinking. Had Mark ever been in trouble with the police before? Only once or twice for minor things, we were told. I could tell that they both knew what we were about to suggest, they thought the same themselves but did not like to admit it; I felt sorry for them. A burglary was one thing, but to steal from your parents! They readily accepted our suggestion about who the obvious suspect was. We arranged to visit again early the following morning and to arrest him then, meanwhile, they would not mention anything about our intended visit.

Shift two was on a quick changeover, and so was I, therefore. We finished at ten in the evening and would be back on duty at six the following morning. It became clear during parade the following morning that there had been several burglaries and attempted burglaries around the industrial estate in Brereton overnight. Dave looked across the table at me, we were both thinking the same thing. It would be interesting to find out what Mark had been up to overnight.

After the customary check of the town centre properties after parade, then breakfast, followed by my customary duty covering the school crossing at a busy crossroads on the A51, I was relieved when Dave picked me up. We set off for Brereton.

Mark was still asleep in bed when his parents let us in. His mother went to wake him up whilst his father told us that Mark had not returned home until three or four in the morning. A few minutes later he came downstairs, rubbing his eyes, still only half awake, to be greeted by two police officers. He denied any knowledge of the metre break when we put the suggestion to him. Despite his denial, Dave arrested him, and we all set off for the

35

police station a few minutes later. After leaving the house, Mark realised that it was obvious, even to him, that he was the only suspect and admitted that he had broken into the metre.

After booking him into the station, we began interviewing him. Dave asked him where the money he had removed was now. He claimed to have spent it all when he went out drinking on his own. It was obvious that he could not have spent all of it on drinks – but he stuck to the story. We pointed out that it would be better if he told us where the rest of the money was, but he just said he had thrown it away. What time did he get home? About three or four in the morning, which corroborated what his parents had said. What had he done between the time the pubs shut and returning home? He said he had wandered about the area. Dave looked at me, and I'm sure he thought this was heading where we both expected it to. Dave mentioned that several premises had been broken into overnight and several more had damage which suggested someone had been trying to break into them, all on the industrial estate *just up the road* from where Mark lived, but he completely denied any knowledge. Despite repeated questioning, he claimed to know nothing about these.

Dave suspended the interview and left, returning a minute later with a CID officer, who then began to question Mark about the break-ins, this time pointing out to him that he was once again the most obvious suspect. Again, he denied any knowledge. We were getting nowhere. I sat throughout this, watching Mark's reaction to their questioning, and thinking. I thought I had got to know Mark a bit more listening to the questioning and watching him. Dave left the office with the CID officer, saying he needed to go and look a few things up. He glanced at me as he left, obviously suggesting I have a chat with Mark.

It was clear to me that Mark was not going to respond to the line of questioning that had been employed so far. I tried something else. I spent a few minutes chatting to Mark about anything but the break-ins, asking him about his life, and his goals – breaking the ice with him. As he relaxed, I gradually began to talk about the burglaries, pointing out the logic of why we all thought he was the main suspect as he had already admitted to one theft! It was a completely innovative approach, and he began to respond. I began scribbling notes on the back of a blank piece of interview paper, as fast as Mark was telling me the details.

By the time Dave returned some minutes later, I was able to tell him that Mark was ready to admit to *all* the burglaries in Brereton overnight. He was also prepared to admit to being responsible for a list of a further fifteen or twenty crimes over the previous month or so. Dave looked at me, astonished. Neither he nor the CID officer had been able to get anywhere with the youth. It did wonders for my reputation on the shift. I was accepted and I had proved myself. It was a much-needed morale booster for me.

Having lived in Rugeley for most of my life, it never ceased to amaze me just what went on below the surface, despite the reputation it had for trouble. I quickly learned that much more goes on than the public ever gets to hear about. On a Saturday, a few weeks later, in early April, I was working nights with my adopted shift. The shift was progressing normally for a Saturday night. A small amount of public order to sort out earlier on, a high-speed car which refused to stop for a foot patrol and a drunk driver that Dave and I picked up. In the early hours of the morning, we were all sitting in the mess room eating our meal. One of the specials who had joined a month or two after I had, was finishing his duty and setting off for home after saying good night to everyone in the mess room.

Ten minutes later he returned to the station; something had happened from his expression as he stuck his head around the mess room door, interrupting our game of cards.

"Sarge, I've found a girl up the road, she's near the entrance of the Vine Pub, I can't get near her, she's hysterical. I think she's been attacked."

We dropped everything. I grabbed my radio, hastily pulled my cap on, grabbed my jacket, and we set off through the back door following the rest of the shift; it was quicker on foot than to drive. We set off up the narrow back streets and a minute later we were outside the Vine. The teenage girl, obviously terrified and in a very distressed state was curled up in the doorway of the now silent and deserted pub. We could not get near to her, despite trying to reassure her that we were police officers, and we were trying to help her.

We eventually got a WPC over from Cannock and she managed to calm the girl down. She said she had been attacked and raped earlier in the evening just down the road by the side of the market hall. The attacker had finished off by urinating over her. It was escalating into a major incident.

The girl was taken back to the station, Cannock was informed, and we set off for the scene of the attack. Sure enough, strewn all over the pavement along the side of the market hall was the evidence of the struggle which had taken place. One of her shoes, her handbag; the contents were strewn all over the pavement, and a damp patch presumably where the attacker had urinated. The sergeant came over and warned us to keep clear, then to find some marker tape and tape the whole area off. No one was to be allowed anywhere near the scene until it had been forensically examined. We set about taping the area off. I spent the next hour standing around guarding the scene whilst the girl was interviewed at the station. There was no one around, no one to keep away. Eventually, I returned to the station, the night sky was slowly turning grey as daylight approached.

After a briefing at the station by the senior officers who had come over from Cannock together with about a dozen other officers (a hugely augmented shift for Rugeley!), we set off to search the area in daylight for any further evidence. Despite searching the whole street between the market hall and the pub, the nearby bus station and surrounding areas, no one found anything of interest. Six o'clock came. And went. I was tired. I was left guarding the scene once more, there were more people about now, so at least I had a scene to guard against unsuspecting members of the public. At eight-thirty, the *scene of crime* officer arrived to examine the scene I had guarded for him. I returned to the station, weary and ready for bed. I left for home at nine, just as most of the population was starting their work for the day.

I found out when I returned to the station to start another night shift later that day, that the girl had argued with her boyfriend. They had fought and she had not been raped, although he had assaulted her and urinated over her. She withdrew her complaint of assault.

Situations and jobs we were involved with rarely turned out as I expected them to. Duties were never predictable. But that was surely one of the attractions of the job. The more experience I gained, the more certain I was that I had found the career I wanted, and I was determined to do well.

Of course, not everything with the job was interesting and exciting. There was lots of paperwork. Arrest someone and you would be stuck indoors drafting reports, statements, and form filling, sometimes for hours. Then there were the regular jobs that had to be done. Like the school crossing patrols.

By now, it had become second nature. Whenever a school crossing warden was off sick or on holiday, we had to cover the crossing point. In the first instance, it would fall to the traffic warden. But if he was off sick, on rest days or leave, or very often there was more than one crossing to cover, then it would usually fall to me. One morning after breakfast I was about to leave the station through the back door to make the crossing patrol in time. Sergeant Lakin called me into the mess room.

"Steve, before you go out, come here a minute."

I stuck my head around the mess room door, puzzled. The rest of the shift was eating their breakfast.

"Are you going up to do the crossing patrol?"

"Yes, Sarge, any problem with that?"

"Well, no, Steve, but have you seen the new force order which came into effect this morning?"

I mentally ran through all the force orders I had seen recently but could not recall anything to do with school crossing patrols. It must have been one I missed.

"No, Sarge..." I replied eventually, my mind blank, and I was worried. Was I about to get into trouble?

"I'm surprised at you Steven; I thought you read all the force orders! Anyway, all people covering crossing patrols now must use the 'lollipop' stick. Even police officers. There's one in my office behind the door, you'd better go and fetch it, we do not want you breaking force orders do we?"

"No, Sarge," I replied hesitantly.

I absolutely did *not* want to use a 'lollipop' stick, I'd look like a prat! But if the new order said so. I didn't know what to do. I hesitated not knowing what to say.

"Well go on Steve, you'd better go and fetch it, or you'll be late!"

I wasn't so certain – something was wrong.

"Are you sure I have to sarge?"

"Steve, if that's what force orders say, then you must. Go and have a look if you don't believe me, but after you get back."

"But sarge! I'll look stupid!"

Something was not right. Then Dave could not stop himself from sniggering. No, something was wrong. Then it struck me. I was not falling for that! There was no way that they would catch me out like that!

"OK, Sarge, I'll check the recent force orders when I get back. I'll risk it without a stick this morning, I'm not falling for that, Sarge!"

I walked out through the back door. Their laughter was abruptly cut short as the door slammed shut behind me. I pulled out my pocket notebook just to double-check that the date was April the first. I set off for my crossing patrol smiling, quite confidently and without a stick.

The crossing point I knew best was a junction on the A51 by-pass where there were traffic lights. This was a busy main road, a dual carriageway at this point. Both halves of the dual carriageway were covered by wardens at the lights, but the council had decided, wisely, that the adjoining road also needed a crossing patrol at the lights. It was a busy junction during the rush hours, and it was made more dangerous by the fact that there was a small access road from a one-way street onto the lights opposite the dual carriageway. The junction was an accident blackspot.

I had got to know the other two crossing patrol wardens quite well over the months. I did not mind covering the crossing, but I was always glad when it was over, and I could get back to real

41

police work! A frequent topic of conversation was the dangerous nature of the junction. It was suggested that the council needed to re-design the layout of the junction to make it safer. Our conversations always ended with us agreeing that before that would happen someone would have to get seriously injured at the junction.

One morning just a couple of weeks later I was on earlies. I was grateful to be out on mobile patrol with Dave. The sergeant radioed for us to pop down to the Eaton Lodge, a pub restaurant on the other side of the town, to collect a prisoner's meal. This was a common chore at Rugeley. Because the station was not big enough to have a canteen, prisoners at the station would be treated to a meal from the pub restaurant, and we would have to collect it.

We set off along the bypass towards the Eaton Lodge. I was grateful not to be covering the crossing for once. I waved to Ken, the traffic warden, and the two crossing wardens on the dual carriageway as we passed. It was ten to nine, just at the busiest period for the crossing. A couple of minutes later we were waiting in the kitchens of the Eaton Lodge where kitchen staff were wrapping the prisoner's breakfasts in cling film for us.

Suddenly my radio crackled. It was Ken; he was shouting into his radio, and he sounded hysterical. I looked at Dave; what was that about? Ken was in trouble, it was not possible to make out what he was saying, but he was obviously in distress. Dave called back into his radio, trying to calm Ken down, and we managed to get out of him that there had been some sort of an accident and to get there quickly. My pulse was racing, it sounded serious. I apologised to the kitchen staff, and we left without the meals; I radioed the station and told them we would go as we were closest. Jumping back into the patrol car we set off back up the road, I turned the blue light on.

Thirty seconds later we were approaching the lights. A bus had pulled over just on our side of the lights on the opposite carriageway. We crossed over onto the other side of the road and Dave pulled the car up in the middle of the road just beyond the bus, stopping any more traffic from coming past on that side. It looked worryingly serious as we jumped out of the car, several people were standing around looking bewildered and shocked. Ken was sitting on a garden wall, very pale. He pointed to the bus. Dave went over. I started to re-direct the traffic which was beginning to pile up at the junction. A brief time later Dave came back, subdued.

"Get blankets out of the boot of the car then go and do your best to cover up the mess under the bus. It will be a valuable experience for you, Steve. Just take a deep breath first. It's Marion, she's been run over by the bus, she's dead." I looked back towards the bus. Marion was one of the crossing wardens I'd waved to just ten minutes before. I knew Marion quite well.

But I had a job to do. I walked over to the car and pulled blankets from the boot. I took a deep breath and walked calmly over onto the pavement. The bus was full of students on their way to Stafford College. They sat silently, stunned by what had happened. I glanced up at the bus, the driver was sitting in a state of shock in his driving seat. I knelt and looked underneath. For the first time, I realised that there was only a small space under a bus. It was not a pleasant sight, but neither was it sickeningly disgusting. What was visible in the few inches of space between the bus and the tarmac was hardly a human being, it wasn't a person any longer and that made it easier. The only thing that made it recognisable was the white and fluorescent yellow overcoat that Marion was wearing, torn into shreds, and scraped onto the tarmac for several yards under the bus. A leg was sticking out at an odd angle from the mass, and the stockings were torn to shreds. It was obvious that Marion must have been about to step onto the safety of the pavement when the bus hit her, so thankfully, she would be completely unaware of what was looming behind her as the bus dragged her under its wheel and it would, thankfully, have been instant.

The most distressing part of the scene was the lollipop stick lying on the tarmac next to the body, curled up and squashed flat, just like a piece of paper when a ruler is dragged over it. Together with her cap which lay on the tarmac a few yards away, it rammed home the fact that what I was looking at really was a person, or had been a person, and what is more, someone whom I knew well. I threw the blankets over the remains, as best I could, to conceal them from nosy members of the public. At least she was owed this dignity. I crawled back onto the pavement and stood up again.

Other patrol cars were arriving, and there was quite a crowd gathering so I spent a few minutes moving people away from the scene. A fire tender arrived, then a couple of ambulances, and the area was taking on the grim spectacle of a serious accident site.

Ken was very shaken; he had seen the accident happen right in front of him. Marion had crossed a group of school kids to the central reservation and was walking back to the safety of the pavement. The bus had come out of the access road opposite, across the junction. The driver was completely unaware that he was heading straight for Marion, he hit her just as she was about to step back onto the pavement.

An empty bus arrived and was parked behind. I stepped on board the service bus and spoke to the shocked and subdued passengers, mostly students going to college. I explained that they should walk to the bus behind which would continue to Stafford, and I warned them not to look under the bus. Without exception, they did, and many became hysterical. Despite my best efforts to cover the body, it was still obvious what was under the blankets.

Within a few minutes, the relief bus left with the passengers, after we had taken details of any witnesses. The visibly upset and shocked bus driver was taken to an ambulance and the fire and rescue service began their grim task of lifting the bus with airbags to remove the remains of the body. I spent the following hour directing the traffic on the by-pass opposite and by eleven-thirty, the scene was clear, apart from a scraped mark on the road which remained for weeks afterwards. Dave and I returned to the station in silence.

Someone had returned the slightly curled lollipop stick to the station; it was propped up outside the control room. Someone with a sick sense of humour had marked an 'x' on it. But then this sort of humour was one way to cope with dealing with these sorts of incidents. I remained detached, even pleased with myself. I had passed another personal hurdle. I had always wondered how I would react to such an incident. I went down to the mess room to join Dave for a cup of coffee. A few minutes later Sgt Lakin called me into his office to thank me for the professional way we had dealt with what was an exceedingly difficult incident. I smiled and thanked him and said I just wanted to sit down for a drink with Dave. I went back to the mess room, it was starting to sink in.

A short time later Sgt Lakin stuck his head around the door and apologetically asked us if we would mind going back up to the junction to cover the crossing there at lunchtime. Both Ken the traffic warden and the other crossing warden had gone off sick, understandably. Now it was down to me and Dave to fill in.

That was the most difficult part of the whole incident; the experience was just beginning to affect both of us, and it was the last place we wanted to be. And the last thing we wanted to do. Nevertheless, the job had to be done. The duty was strange, the scene seemed so normal. Apart from that mark on the tarmac. News of the accident had spread fast, and most of the kids and adults who crossed asked about it. Both Dave and I were glad when we could leave and return to the station half an hour later.

After the shift had finished, I left for home. However, the full effects of the incident were only just beginning to affect me, and they lasted for several weeks afterwards. Whenever I walked from home into town, I would cross the by-pass quite close to the scene of the accident. I became worried to an unusual degree about crossing the road there, waiting sometimes two or three minutes until I was completely certain it was safe to cross, and with no approaching vehicles for at least two or three hundred yards in either direction. As a direct result of this accident, the junction was subsequently altered and the access road onto it was closed. Our prediction had come true.

Not everything I dealt with was grim or disturbing. Just as unpredictably, what initially might have seemed like something serious would end up having a much lighter, even humorous element to it.

Less than a week after the fatal road accident I was on patrol with Ian Gilbey, another officer on my adopted shift whom I got on very well with. I became worried when we were diverted to a reported fire in the back garden of a house on the road where I live. It quickly became clear that it was on the other side and several houses up the street from where I lived, to my relief.

The fire tender had already been there several minutes when

we arrived, and the fire had already been extinguished. We followed the water hoses into the back garden. A handful of fire officers and a very embarrassed neighbour of mine were standing around surveying the scene. A neat path ran up the centre of the garden, passing through a row of four tall conifer trees halfway up the garden. Or three tall conifer trees and a black, smoking stick twenty feet tall, in the middle. I turned to my neighbour who explained, sheepishly, that he had merely been trying to burn away the weeds around the base of the tree. He went on to tell us that he had intended to remove that tree sometime in the future to let in more light. Ian, in his dry and humorous way, pointed the obvious out, that he had achieved both of those aims in one go before we left to spare him any further embarrassment.

Even crimes that we attended could have their humorous side. One evening just a month later I was on mobile patrol with Dave. We were diverted to a card shop in the town centre where a window had been smashed, and the offender was still outside! Not far away, we were there within a minute. The window of the shop was broken, shards of glass lying on the pavement for several yards around.

As we pulled up outside the shop, a tall youth aged about nineteen who was standing a few yards away, ran off towards the Market Square. We jumped out of the car and ran after the youth. Dave caught him as he ran across the far side of the market square and arrested him. A 'Garfield' stuffed toy, taken from the shop, fell out of his jacket to his acute embarrassment. He had no choice but to admit the crime! He was taken to the station, interviewed, and charged with the damage and the theft.

Two days later I was leaving the station in a patrol car with Joe, another officer from my shift. I was in the middle of describing the 'Garfield Case' to Joe when, to my amazement and as if to demonstrate, the same youth ran across the road in front of us causing Joe to brake sharply. Under his arm was a Garfield toy! He ran off up a one-way street opposite.

"That's him!" I shouted, pointing to the fast-disappearing youth. Joe turned the car into the street, and we drove past the youth and pulled up just beyond him. He knew he had been caught again and to my relief, he slowed to a walk. I wouldn't have to chase him. I opened the rear door for him and invited him to jump in. Which he did.

I finished the first phase of my formal training and sat the phase one exam at headquarters. I was incredibly pleased when I passed it in the top grade. It reinforced my belief that I had, at last, found my chosen career and everybody I worked with at the station agreed. My confidence was increasing rapidly, I had successfully worked through my probationary period, and I was being let out to patrol on my own, I had been a police officer for over a year.

An incident a few weeks later, in mid-June, reminded me just how potentially dangerous police work could be. It also did wonders for the reputations of Ian Gilbey and me, around the station. We were diverted, mid-evening, to a licensed club on one of the council estates where the licensee was complaining about a customer who was being a nuisance. He would be drunk, I thought as we made our way.

The customer in question was outside the pub when we pulled up; the licensee pointed him out to us. He was big. At least six feet tall and very muscular. And he was drunk; his balance was not good. I did not fancy arguing with him without help. Neither did Ian, from his expression as we pulled up. "Oh, no!"

But we did argue with him. He insisted on going back into the club. Ian tactfully suggested he might be better off going home. But his reply was quite emphatic:

"You can't fuckin' make me go home; I'll go home when I fuckin' want to." So, we knew where we stood. Several of the club customers came out to watch the entertainment. I looked at Ian, we had no choice. Ian took hold of him and informed him, tactfully, that he was under arrest. To my relief, Sgt Lakin with another special arrived to help. Despite a lot of swearing, and threats the man was persuaded, again tactfully, to get into the back of our patrol car. I sat in the back with him on the journey back to the station. A few yards down the road he became aggressive again and without warning lunged for Ian, putting his massive arms around the driver's seat. Ian braked sharply and pulled up. I struggled to pull him off, but between us we managed, remarkably easily, to place a pair of handcuffs on him.

Despite a lot of swearing and abuse, we got him back to the station. He remained aggressive so he was 'invited' to step straight into the cell. I was relieved when the cell door banged shut. Then the 'entertainment' began. The man became even more aggressive, hurling himself at the cell door, screaming, kicking, and punching. We locked the steel gate at the end of the cell corridor – just to be safe. He was still hurling himself around when we handed over to the night shift half an hour later.

I was shocked but not surprised to see the extent of his destructive powers the following afternoon. The heavy-duty, solid oak, steel-plated, re-enforced cell door was going to have to be replaced, it was hanging off its hinges at a funny angle. The cast iron spy-hole surround was smashed into several pieces. Ian looked at the fragments thoughtfully as I passed them to him when he turned up for work a few minutes after me. Other officers were coming up and patting us on the back, looking at us with a degree of awe!

Chapter 4

The Obscene Excuse

As the summer progressed, I continued regular duties, gaining experience and my confidence grew that I would be able to make a good career within the police service. I wanted just a bit more experience, now out of probation, working on my own initiative, and then I would put in an application to the regular force.

One pleasant diversion over the summer was the news that Nitin's brother was getting married. Nitin was my friend who had moved to London to work for the BBC. I was invited to the reception after the wedding ceremony at a village hall a few miles from Rugeley. It was a warm and sunny August afternoon, and I had a wonderful time meeting some of Nitin's family.

I would have normally been working nights with my shift, but I had booked it off, and I had told the sergeant that I would not be able to make it. Shift two had come to rely on me being around, I was just another bobby on the shift. Sgt Lakin was continually thanking me for my contribution to the shift, but as I kept pointing out to him, I was gaining as much experience as possible to get into the regulars and besides, I enjoyed working with them. It was satisfying and a huge confidence booster to be considered as just another member of the shift!

After the wedding reception, a few of us returned to Rugeley to continue the celebrations at one of the pubs in the town. We had an enjoyable evening, but thankfully, as I soon realised, I had hardly anything alcoholic to drink. Nitin brought along one of his cousins who had travelled up from Devon, and we had an enjoyable time chatting. Eventually, we made ready to leave the pub as it was already the last orders and it had been a long but very enjoyable day.

There was a lot of noise as we stepped outside into the warm evening air. I stopped and listened. It was coming from the street just around the corner, from outside a wine bar, (the town had lots of pubs and bars), where we could all hear a lot of people shouting and chanting in the street. I soon realised it was starting to get a bit out of hand and I was concerned for my friends; we were only a couple of hundred yards from the taxi rank though.

The wine bar was a popular flashpoint for trouble in the town. As we reached the corner, I became concerned; the trouble was much worse than I had thought. About fifty people were milling around the entrance and in the road, obviously very drunk and looking for trouble. My thoughts were racing; my shift was on duty, and I knew there were only three or four officers, including Sgt Lakin, who was available to go out on patrol, one police car was already there on the other side of the crowd, I could not see who it was, but I was concerned for their safety. And ours. This was potentially the worst public order situation I had yet seen in the town. I made a quick decision.

Both Nitin and his cousin were alarmed at what was happening. I pointed them in the direction of the taxi rank and after waiting for a minute to check they had arrived there safely; I ran around to the station via a circuitous route. The station was deserted apart from Di, the WPC on control, but there was a lot of noise coming from the control room; there was a lot of radio traffic. I let myself in and told Di that I was coming on duty to help. I phoned home and asked my father to collect me from the station straight away.

Ten minutes later I was home getting changed and five minutes after was back at the station booking out a personal radio. I grabbed my tunic and gloves and set out, heading towards where I could hear the chanting and shouting which was moving away from the area of the wine bar. It became steadily more intimidating as I approached the source.

It was clear that the main body of troublemakers was moving up towards Horsefair at the top of the town. Two minutes later I approached Horsefair with some caution. The atmosphere was electric; the crowd had grown to nearer one hundred and more police reinforcements were turning up as I spoke. Patrols were being directed to Rugeley from all over the county.

I spotted Sgt Lakin and made a beeline for him. He seemed pleased to see me, and I was certainly pleased to see him and the rest of the shift. He thanked me for coming on at short notice, I was not expected after all. The shift stood around in a small group near the traffic island, the main body of trouble was a hundred yards further up Horsefair, but there were isolated groups of drunken youths and individuals who were milling around the area, and more were turning up all the while. Trouble was spreading down into the town centre too.

Sgt Lakin seemed concerned, and he turned to me.

"Steve, go back to the station, I'm worried that there's only Di on her own in there, she might need backup. Watch how you go, call up if there's any trouble."

"OK, Sarge, good luck!" I set off back the way I had come. Certainly, now, there were even more people about, the tension was spreading over the whole of the town centre and there was a brooding, ominous atmosphere. I was glad of the safety of the station as the door closed behind me and Di was pleased that I was back.

From the radio transmissions we were listening to, the tension was still building, fights had broken out, and an arrest had been made. Patrols from the farthest reaches of the county were arriving by now. Then a message sent a chill through me that I will never forget. Sgt Lakin called the station.

"Six four to Whisky Bravo! Has Steve got back to the station yet?" he shouted into his radio against the din.

"Yes, he's here…"

"Good, just to let you know, the crowd are on the move, they're heading for the police station! We're on our way down Elmore Lane, we should get there first, but make sure all the windows are shut…over!"

We looked at each other, quite shocked. I jumped onto the table and looked down the street. No one was in sight but, I could already hear the roar getting louder and the screamed obscenities and chanting becoming rapidly more distinct, so I pushed the window up and locked it. My pulse was racing. I was extremely glad that it was an old, solidly built and secure building! I ran into the Sarge's office, the parade room and the inspectors' office to make sure all the windows were closed; they were. Then straight back to the control room.

Our 'troops' arrived, to our relief, just before the mass of seething obscenities arrived from the town centre; scuffles broke out straight away and within a few seconds there was absolute mayhem outside the station.

Suddenly there was a commotion in the entrance passage, I looked through the public hatch. Two or three bobbies were struggling with a youth who had been arrested, and other youths were trying to force their way in to help their mate. I ran around to the door and pulled it open, revealing the struggling mass.

Between us we dragged the youth, stinking strongly of alcohol, in through the door which then slammed reassuringly shut behind us. The youth was dragged, still screaming obscenities and struggling, straight down to the cell block. There was no time for the formalities of booking him in now, he was pushed into the cell and the door slammed shut. I made my way back towards the entrance. Yet another youth was being dragged in, again I opened the door and took hold of the screaming and struggling youth. Yet again he was pushed into a cell. The bell rang for the rear custody office door. I grabbed the keys and ran down into the charge room and could hear a commotion outside the back door. Thankfully, there was a few seconds of respite to catch my breath as I looked for the right key and unlocked the door.

Several struggling bodies almost fell into the charge room as the door burst open, two youths had been arrested and were being restrained. Again, they were dragged kicking and screaming straight around to the cells.

I ran back up to the control room, the noise outside had hardly abated. The phone rang. An irate female complaining about a noisy party in their neighbour's house. I took the details and politely explained we were too busy at present but would be around as soon as we could spare an officer. Yet again I could hear officers struggling in the passageway. I replaced the handset ran around, and once again spent a breathless minute struggling with the youth as he was dragged to a cell.

The noise within the station was fast becoming worse than the noise outside, the volume on the radio base stations was turned up and the radio traffic was constant; Di, on control was struggling to keep up. Those ringleaders who were now holed up in the cells and detention rooms for their troubles were screaming and banging on the doors. The passageway door suddenly opened, and Sgt Lakin came in looking slightly dishevelled and out of breath. He went straight down towards the charge room where more officers were waiting at the back door with a prisoner.

The phone rang again, the same irate woman complaining now about our lack of attention. I restrained myself. I explained that we were still extremely busy but would get around as soon as possible and replace the handset before she could insult me further. There was no time to argue with people like that now. Noise within the station was growing in intensity with every prisoner, who was placed in any available secure space we could find. Then, as suddenly as it had erupted outside the station, the drunken mass broke up, and the ringleaders were now locked up. Groups of rowdy drunken youths disappeared into the night. Around fifteen were now locked up in the station which almost seemed to heave and groan as they vented their hatred on anyone within earshot.

The phone rang again. Somebody was woken up by a group of youths fighting outside their house on one of the estates. The other phone rang with another report of trouble on another of the estates. A message flashed on the computer screen from the control room at headquarters which had received a 999 call about yet another fight. The main riot had been broken up, only to fragment into smaller groups which had fanned out all over the estates around the town. Patrols were hurriedly despatched and a few minutes later the bell rang in the custody office. Two or three other youths were dragged kicking and screaming to join their drunken friends in the cells. By twelve-thirty, only an hour after the trouble erupted on Horsefair, the superintendent who had come over from Cannock to take charge of the situation decided it was all over and called a de-briefing in the parade room.

A mass of panting, exhausted and dishevelled officers piled into the station and made for the parade room. I was dispatched to guard the police vehicles left parked outside. On my own.

I pulled my tunic on, picked up my radio and checked that it was working before I left the station. I took a deep breath and pushed open the door to the outside world. The silence was almost eerie. The atmosphere of calm and the ordinary noise of the town at this time in the morning – just the distant sound of the occasional passing vehicle on the main road – made it difficult to believe that the mayhem of only a few minutes before had happened.

The tiny parking area in front of the station, just big enough for the usual one or two police vehicles parked on it, was crammed with four. Police vehicles of every description – patrol cars, traffic cars, vans, motorbikes and carriers, were parked along both sides of the road for a hundred yards in either direction or those which did not fit were parked in the pedestrianised street opposite.

I stood and waited, thankful that the station, full of bobbies, was only a few feet away. A young couple passing on their way home, completely unaware of the events they had only just missed being in the middle of, walked past in amazement. I wished them good night as they passed. Rugeley had rarely seen so many police vehicles!

Eventually, I was called back into the station and asked to resume patrol with a dog handler who had travelled down from Stoke. He did not know Rugeley and wanted a navigator. There were still isolated reports of disturbances around the town. We set off on patrol in his van, and I was relieved we had a dog in the back. Thankfully, we soon discovered the town was resuming its normal quiet state for this time in the morning.

We were driving down one of the lanes on the far side of the town a few minutes later when a radio message diverted my companion to a report of trouble flaring up outside one of the nightclubs in Stafford, eight miles away. There was no time to drop me back at the station, so I found myself on my way to Stafford at high speed!

Ten minutes later as we were near the nightclub, we drove straight into the middle of a crowd of about a hundred drunken revellers spilling out all over the road, and with some careful driving, we parked in a side street. Once again, the atmosphere was electric with tension, I was in the middle of a potential riot for the second time in an evening. It was very reassuring to have a dog with us though!

The main crowd were a hundred yards up the road but there were still groups of hostile youths all around. We stood in the welcome recess of a shop doorway, the police dog snarling and straining in his leash, sensing the atmosphere. A foolhardy group of drunken youths walked towards us and began their ritual taunting. My colleague warned them not to step any closer and as if to illustrate, the dog barked and began snarling menacingly, baring its sharp teeth. The youths, sober enough to realise the danger of their taunting, backed off. I smiled.

We waited for the tension to break, but slowly, unlike the confrontation in Rugeley, the tension died down, and the crowds began to dissipate. The swift and overwhelming police presence illustrated the futility of any trouble even to the half-dazed, alcohol-soaked brains staggering past. There would be no riot in Stafford. Not tonight, at least.

At three-thirty, I was dropped off outside Rugeley police station, relieved and very tired. I was glad that there had been no more trouble in the town whilst I had been off on my adventure in Stafford. After a bite to eat, I went out on patrol with Ed, but the shift ended quietly. At six I booked off duty, exhausted.

It was amazing how such an incident could develop, unexpectedly. There had been no warning that any major problems existed, yet it all seemed to unfold just from a small group of angry, drunken youths spoiling for a fight as they spilt out of the wine bar. I went to sleep relieved that no one had been seriously injured and there did not appear to be any damage.

The following evening at ten I paraded for duty for the last night duty of a month. There was a degree of tension in the parade room, yet the evening passed quietly with no incidents of any note.

Yet again, a week of nights had proved just how unpredictable police work could be. There were no further outbreaks of public disorder on the same scale, and the town resumed its normal, much quieter composure.

I was asked a week later by my section officer if I would break from my usual pattern of working with shift two to parade for a special duty the following Sunday morning; there was going to be a sports day organised by the youth centre on the playing fields and I was needed to help control the traffic entering the field.

By now I realised that Sundays could often be the most unpredictable day of the week to work. Friday and Saturday evenings would be expected to produce some public disorder, and Monday mornings would be the burglaries which had been discovered when businesses re-opened after the weekend. Sundays were completely unpredictable and sometimes could be the busiest day of the week. On top of that, because of the way the shift system worked, only two shifts would cover the period from six on Sunday morning until six the following morning.

Each shift was split in two and staggered, half starting at six and the rest at ten. Therefore, the period from six until ten on Sunday mornings and the period from two until six on Monday mornings would be staffed by only half a shift.

I was not surprised, therefore, when I walked into the station at half-past nine on Sunday morning that the station was almost empty. There was only the controller, Trevor in the station, the other officer on duty was out on patrol. There seemed to be some radio dialogue between the two, there was a job 'on the go' but otherwise, the station was quiet.

I dropped my bag in the drying room, changed into my uniform, and walked down to the control room to book a radio out. There was a pleasant, relaxed atmosphere about the day, it was sunny and going to be quite warm again. Trevor was still speaking to Simon over the radio. Trevor turned and greeted me as I walked in, I asked what had happened overnight, but it had been quiet. Simon had gone out to investigate a report of a body in the stream along the edge of the playing field where I was about to go myself for the sports day. A young lad had called at the station a few minutes before and reported seeing what looked like a body, Trevor was telling me. Simon was just going to check that it was a mistake, just some rubbish or something, as was usually the case with these types of reports. I picked up a radio of my own and was clipping the battery on when Simon called the station again.

There *was* the body of a woman in the stream, it looked like she had been assaulted, and she was virtually naked. I looked at Trevor. Simon said he urgently needed someone else there to help preserve the scene. I wasted no time. Pulling my jacket on I ran out of the back door and set off through the narrow streets and through the park to the playing fields on the other side of the by-pass. As they say, the shit had just hit the fan.

The patrol car was parked at the entrance of a driveway into a field next to the stream. There was a steep, wooded hillside, below which was the stream and beyond that the playing fields. Simon had already put some marker tape across the gateway. As I crossed the road to join him other patrols arrived from Cannock. More were on their way; a major incident was unfolding.

I ducked under the tape and found Simon; I could see the body lying half in the stream on the nearside bank below, it was a pathetic scene. It was within sight of the by-pass only fifty yards away. As I stood talking to Simon other patrols turned up, and I was despatched to guard the top end of the field. I had a funny feeling that my day was not going to turn out as I had expected. It was highly unlikely, anyway, that the sports day on the field next to the stream would be allowed to go ahead now. It was cancelled soon after.

I found a convenient position at the top of the field where I had an unobstructed view of the events as they unfolded and began the task of keeping nosy spectators away from the scene. And the bloody journalists trying to get into the field.

For the second time in a fortnight, the town saw an influx of police vehicles. The day passed very slowly; I was glad that it was pleasantly warm at least. By lunchtime, the body had been removed but the scenes of crime officers carried on with their search of the area. Six hours after I had arrived at the field, I was allowed a break; a meal had been organised for all officers on duty at the incident, at the 'Little Chef' café down the road. I returned to my position with some reluctance half an hour later, wondering when I would be allowed to return to the station! The operation was wound down at teatime, but I was asked to remain on guard with one or two other officers until they could find replacements from Cannock. I stood and talked to Ian Gilbey. I was beginning to wonder whether I would finish in time for the drink I had planned with some of my friends from the caving group later!

The sun sank lower in the sky, then set. It grew darker and eventually at just after nine we were relieved of our positions by officers from Cannock. I walked back to the station with Ian, booked off duty after having been at the scene for almost twelve hours, and made my way to the pub for a well-earned and much-needed drink.

It turned out that the woman, who lived locally, had been sexually assaulted and strangled. I was back on duty the following afternoon with my shift and was in the control room when the CID was out waiting for the suspected murderer to arrive, unsuspecting, home from work. There was a chase on foot as officers moved in, relayed over the radio to all the officers crammed eagerly around the control room radio base station, there was a huge cheer as the suspect was caught and arrested a few minutes later.

I spent a fascinating afternoon some weeks later with the suspect handcuffed to me in the dock of the crowded courtroom where the committal hearing was held. After a tense few minutes, whilst the magistrates made their decision and I waited with the suspect in the cells below, he was committed for trial. At the later trial, he was found guilty of murder and sentenced to life.

I was pleased when a couple of weeks after the murder I was asked by my section officer if I would tutor a new special who was joining and would be down for his first duty later in the evening. It was a good sign of the progress I was making; I was now in a position where I was going to be teaching policing to someone who would be relying on me totally when we went out on patrol, exactly the position I had been in fourteen months earlier. I returned to the station to meet the recruit at eight-thirty, the section officer had already shown him around the station. I was pleasantly surprised to be introduced to Steve Smith whom I had last met eighteen months earlier when I had sat my entrance exam at headquarters. So, he had made it as a police officer, at last!

After a chat, I took Steve out on patrol around the town centre, and we got on very well. We called into the Prince of Wales pub for a drink and a chat when we finished at ten. Steve told me he had seen me standing in the field the day of the murder a couple of weeks earlier but could not get across to me to tell me he had got in at last. We arranged to meet on duty again two days later, on Saturday afternoon. I spent the first part of that afternoon on patrol with Dave, Steve was coming on later. I was called back to the station to pick up Steve at three-thirty and we spent a pleasant couple of hours walking around the town centre, I was teaching Steve as much as I could about The Job.

At five Dave called me on the radio; he was being sent to a report of a domestic argument at a house in Brereton and wanted some backup just in case…

We met Dave at Globe Island a minute later and jumped into the car. This was the first time Dave had met Steve. They would end up, as Steve and I were becoming, good mates. This was the first potential incident of any note that Steve had been to. Dave said it would be unwise for us to go in too heavy-handed, and it would be better if Steve stopped in the car. I suggested it might be best if I waited instead, as it would be a good experience for Steve.

A minute later we pulled up outside the house. Dave and Steve got out and set off up the path whilst I settled down to write up my pocket notebook entry for the afternoon. I glanced up; they had gone inside leaving the front door ajar. I hated domestics. They were messy incidents, never straightforward like public disorder incidents, and both parties expected you to take their side.

I looked up again, Steve was shouting at me and waving his arms frantically from the front door. Something was wrong. I jumped out of the car, leapt over the garden gate, and ran up the path. I followed Steve back into the house, and there was an obvious commotion.

What I saw when I entered was awful. Dave was being pinned to the back of the settee by a violent bloke who had his hands around Dave's throat, his face was turning blue. The bastard! No one was going to get away with treating my mate like that, I pushed past Steve and hurled myself at the bloke.

The settee fell over backwards, and we all fell in a heap on the floor behind. I frantically pulled at the assailant and punched him hard between the shoulder blades; it did the trick. He let go of Dave, who managed to get some leverage – and his breath back. Steve came over and between us, we managed to restrain and handcuff the bloke who was dragged kicking and screaming to the patrol car. Steve had his first experience of aggression.

Afterwards, Dave thanked me for, as he saw it, saving his life! Steve could have alerted me by the radio as soon as it had all blown up, but he was learning, and in the panic he never, understandably, even thought of that.

Over the following months, we became good friends, we got on well and Steve was as keen as I was to get on in the specials and make a career in the regulars. He ran a car repair business from a garage at the end of a street near the town centre, and his garage became a regular tea stop when I was on foot patrol.

As far as the specials were concerned, my work so far had gone much better than I dared hope it might, it was about time I thought about applying to the regulars. I was frustrated that although I was enjoying myself immensely, I needed a career with a regular decent income. I was also becoming increasingly frustrated that I did not have a partner, I was in some respects, very lonely.

Since joining the specials, I had fitted in well, out of necessity, with the other bobbies I worked with. Quite commonly, parades would be interrupted whilst all the 'men' on the shift gawped at and commented on any attractive female who walked past. I feigned joining in, though it was awkward and I hated doing it. Out on patrol with other officers, especially with my mate Dave, it was even more clear. And even more difficult to lie. It showed me that my own love life was non-existent. But what could I do about it? I could not talk to my mates in the police. How could I find someone in a similar position who I got on with?

I could not help noticing, whilst idly flicking through a police magazine in the station one day, a small advertisement for a gay and lesbian police association. I thought about it and made a mental note to contact it sometime. I was feeling increasingly isolated because of my sexuality, though I could never say anything to my colleagues. I was leafing through a local newspaper one day when a solution to my loneliness leapt out at me. In answer to some anonymous person in a similar position who had written to the agony aunt, was a contact for a gay dating agency. I wrote the number and the address on a scrap of paper and soon after plucked up the courage to contact the agency. They sent a form back which I returned with the joining fee and waited eagerly for the first replies.

After a lot of encouragement from the shift and my sergeant, I phoned the recruiting department at headquarters and asked them to send me an application form for the regulars. I filled it in and sent it back. My life was beginning to move forward at last.

Over the following few weeks, I was sent, and rejected, several contacts with other gay men. It was frustrating that most had nothing in common with me. But then, after one such contact, I met Mike in the spring of 1989. We got on very well at our first meeting in Birmingham and over the following few weeks, we spoke regularly on the phone and met as often as possible. Even though Mike came to visit me at home, I was incredibly careful that my parents would not realise the truth about us, I was not ready to tell them, I could not do that.

We spent a weekend camping in the Peak District during the spring, I showed Mike around the Manifold Valley where I had spent so much time exploring caves. We got on very well and quickly became close friends.

My application to the regulars was taking its time, even though I was already an employee of Staffordshire Police. Eventually, several months later I had a phone call inviting me for an interview at headquarters. I was there! I was reassured by Sgt Lakin, the station inspector, and other senior officers from Cannock that I would walk into the job; the interview was going to be a formality. I spent the evenings I was free running and getting myself physically fit. Since joining I had spent many thousands of hours on duty, experienced every type of incident and proved to my satisfaction and that of other officers in the division that I was more than capable of performing the job effectively. In the meantime, I continued my regular duties. A duty in late June once again showed how dangerous the job could be.

It was late one Monday evening, the first duty of a week of nights. A report of a domestic in Handsacre, a village three miles out of town, sent me and Jeff to sort it out. Fortunately, another patrol car was nearby and waited outside, just in case.

We walked into a tense but subdued and to our immediate relief, calm atmosphere. The middle-aged man who showed us in, we then realised was holding a sword, I was wary of it and kept my eye on him. His son, Craig, was sitting on a chair in the sitting room, crying, blood streaming down his face. His father pointed to the kitchen we had passed on the way in.

"It's my other son, Chris, he caused the fight. I want him out."

Jeff told the older man to put the sword down somewhere out of the way. We walked back up the passageway and into the kitchen. A man in his thirties, very drunk and holding a half-empty pint glass of beer was standing by the sink. He glared silently at us as we stepped in. I stood back and used my radio to ask the other officers to come inside quietly. I became acutely aware of all the sharp knives I could see lying around the kitchen and together with the sword we had seen on our way in, this was altogether a much more dangerous situation than we had initially thought, and the atmosphere was tense.

The old man stuck his head around the door and pointed his finger towards his son.

"I want him out."

Craig was in the passage behind, and an argument was rapidly escalating again. Chris was becoming quite aggressive; I was quite concerned for the safety of everyone around. Jeff intervened.

"Chris, your father has asked you to leave his house – come on, why not go?" But Chris became aggressive again.

"No! I will not go! I'll kill him if you do not arrest me!"

"Stop being stupid, we do not want to arrest you, you're just making things worse for yourself." I intervened.

Chris waved the half-full glass of beer menacingly towards us in between taking huge gulps from it. We were losing our patience. Jeff broke the tension again.

"Put the drink down and leave the house!" Chris remained aggressive.

"You may as well take me because I'm gonna kill him!"

Suddenly his whole attitude changed. He stepped backwards and held the glass out towards us in a threatening manner.

"Come on, get me then!"

Despite protestations from us to leave the house, Chris remained aggressive and backed into a passageway at the rear of the kitchen. I looked at Jeff and we walked forward towards him, following him into the passage. He backed right up to a rear doorway as we advanced slowly towards him, my pulse was racing.

Jeff suddenly lunged forward and took a firm hold of Chris's left arm but he managed to jerk the glass up against Jeff's neck; this was desperate! I pushed forward and between us, we managed to force the glass out of Chris' hand; it dropped onto the floor and smashed. Chris was quickly handcuffed, to our great relief, and finally led out to the car.

Once again, I had seen just how unpredictable and dangerous police work could sometimes be. But it did not put me off. My interview was already only a day or two away. Sgt Lakin offered me some pre-interview advice and asked me to call in at the station before driving over to headquarters, on the morning I had the interview.

I called in, slightly nervous about the interview ahead of me.

Sgt Lakin reassured me everything would be OK and led me to a spare office upstairs. We spent half an hour going over the questions he believed they would ask, and the answers I should give. Before leaving he wished me good luck. I set off for Stafford.

The first part of the morning was the physical tests. It was not too difficult, but I had been training for a few weeks. That was the first hurdle over. I was confident as I walked into the interview room to face the three senior officers later that morning.

I was surprised by how closely the questioning followed the pattern that Sgt Lakin had described. I gave the right answers and was relieved that by the end of it, I appeared to have performed well, it was not as gruelling as some had led me to believe. I sat outside nervously awaiting their decision. A few minutes later I was invited back in.

I was turned down. I sat staring incredulously at the officers who sat smiling impassively. I could not believe what they had said.

"Why, for what reason?" was all I could ask.

They fumbled, nervously, with the papers they had in front of them, and one looked up to answer.

"Because, Mr Johnson, you haven't proved to us that you are capable of holding down a paid job."

I stared back at them, disbelieving what I'd just heard, but that was it, the end of the story. Goodbye.

I walked out of the building in a state of shock. I was both upset and angry. It did not make any sense, and the reason they gave was an obscene insult since I had given them two years of full-time support – for little pay. What more could I have done? What better commitment could anyone have given?

I drove back to Rugeley police station to break the news to my friends and colleagues there – my shift was still on duty. I could not stand the thought that I had to go and break the news to my parents. Why the hell should I give Staffordshire Police one more bloody second of my spare time?

I arrived back at the station a few minutes later still shocked and upset. I walked in through the back door, not over-eager to break the news. Joe was in the parade room with his head buried in piles of self-generated paperwork, as usual. He looked up.

"Well, how did it go?"

"They rejected me." Joe stared at me and smiled.

"You're joking – stop pulling my leg! When do you start?"

"I'm not joking." He stared at me; the smile vanished.

"What reason did they give?"

"Because I haven't got a paid job. They said I had not shown them I could hold down a bloody paid job!" my anger was boiling over, "the bloody bastards!"

I sat down, shaking. Joe echoed my sentiments. He called through to the sergeant's office.

"Sarge! are you there? Come through here."

Sgt Lakin walked through and spotted me; his face lit up.

"Well, Steve, when are you leaving us then?"

I could not say anything, I was in a state of shock, and I had to control myself. Joe answered for me.

"They turned him down because he has not proved to them that he can hold down a paid job."

"You're pulling my leg…"

"No," I answered, looking up.

Sgt Lakin walked across, pulled a chair up next to me and sat down.

"Go and make us all a drink, Joe." He said calmly. Joe got

up and left the room.

"Go on Steve, tell us what happened." His voice was calming and supportive, just what I desperately needed right then. I told him how the interview had gone, what questions they had asked and how I thought I had answered them correctly. He shook his head, unable, as I was, to take in what had happened. I still had to go home and break the news to my parents. I sat in the parade room going over it all with Joe and the Sarge, feeling very much supported. I finished my coffee. Eventually, I got up to reluctantly go home, but Sgt Lakin stopped me.

"Steve, I know how you must be feeling now. I wouldn't personally blame you if you never came on duty again. No one here would. But I just want you to know that I hope you don't pack it in. You will be missed. You are an excellent police officer despite what they have told you at headquarters. I would have you on my shift any day in preference to a lot of the idiots who get in these days."

"Thanks, Sarge." It was all I could bring myself to say.

As I got up to leave, a thought which had been forming kept me back. I turned back to Sgt Lakin.

"Sarge, I know this sounds daft, but it seems to me that the reason they gave was an excuse – that it wasn't the real reason…"

Sgt Lakin looked at me for several seconds before replying.

"That's how I see it too. In fact, I'm certain it *was* an excuse."

I pulled the car up on the drive a few minutes later. My mother came running out of the house to hear the news, smiling and eager.

Chapter 5

The Catalyst

I did return to the station, straight away, the following day. The support I received from my colleagues and even senior officers from Cannock was overwhelming. Even the divisional Chief Superintendent offered his support and was surprised at my rejection and their reason. My mother was contacted by a chief inspector from Cannock whom I had never even met, who was genuinely concerned when he heard what had happened. He hoped I would not resign. Everyone agreed it was an obscene decision. Many now believed it was so stupid a reason that it had to be an excuse. It was not the real reason. But no one could find any more out.

I resumed duties, encouraged by the outpouring of genuine support I got. I decided I would at least give it a few more months to see if I could sort out the issue, and if that failed, I would apply to another force, and I would leave Staffordshire. Anyway, I could not just walk out now, it had become a major part of my life. My friends were all in the Job. I could not give it up.

Ironically, just a week or two later I more than proved my worth as a police officer. I was asked one morning to turn up in plain clothes for an initiative that had hastily been arranged to try and catch some car thieves who had recently targeted car parks in Rugeley.

I spent the morning sitting in a car with a regular officer from one of the other shifts. The duty was boring; I was frustrated that he was not interested in the job at hand, he was just wasting time, waiting for the time we could head back to the station. It was a balmy day, especially sitting in a car. Eventually, late in the morning, we returned to the station. It was still only just after midday. It wasn't worth going home to change, we would be finishing at two. I asked Sgt Lakin if he minded if I went out on the town in plain clothes. He had no objection and thought it might be a clever idea – and he was right.

Ten minutes later I left the station again, my radio tucked discreetly into my inside jacket pocket and my 'cuffs in my back pocket. I was relieved to be free, on my own again.

Walking around the town centre out of uniform, but on duty and with radio contact to the station and other officers if I needed it, was liberating. I could wander around, watching for shoplifters or troublemakers, but without being spotted so easily. I knew I had help to hand if I needed it. I could be as nosy as I liked, officially.

I wandered around the town centre enjoying the freedom of being out of uniform. Not that I didn't enjoy police work in uniform; I was proud of the job I did, and I wore my uniform with pride. I looked down at my watch, it was already a quarter to two, time to think about going in, but I was enjoying myself!

I sauntered down the street towards the market square. The town was buzzing with people. Standing for a minute on the corner of a street, watching people going by, my attention suddenly fell on two young men, in their early twenties. Something about them made them stand out from the crowd, my intuition alerted me something was wrong with them. They were both smartly dressed in matching silver-grey suits and carried an empty Argos carrier bag, which was odd. And we did not have

72

an Argos in the town. I didn't recognise them; they were not local. I knew instantly that they were up to no good. I mentally took in their details as they walked right past, within a couple of feet of me, and continued up a side street. I stood watching, as casually as possible, as if I were waiting for someone.

An alarm bell was ringing in my head; I remembered that we had received intelligence reports of two smartly dressed men, like the ones I'd just seen, visiting Woolworths stores around the Midlands, and stealing handfuls of LPs. Barbara, the manager of our own Woolworths had only stopped a similar incident just in time a few days earlier. The side entrance of Woolworths was only a few yards up the side street the two men were walking along. My pulse rate quickened. I stood, casually looking up Albion Street and, just as I expected, I watched them walk into the side entrance of Woolworths.

I turned and ran back around the corner and into the front main entrance of the store, slowing to an innocent stroll as I frantically scanned the shop floor for the two men and for the manager. Barbara was nowhere to be seen, I walked up through the store and spotted the two men walking towards me, towards where the LPs were. Walking casually past them, I made for the checkout counter beyond. The two men walked across to the record department. I whispered to the girl on the counter, whom I knew and told her to find Barbara quickly, I nodded in the direction of the record displays. She understood and walked quickly off to fetch Barbara.

Walking back into the main shop I wandered down an aisle, browsing, watching the two men who were looking around nervously. I was not sure whether they had become suspicious of me, but they lost their nerve, suddenly walking past me quickly, out of the entrance they had entered a minute or two before. I set off after them, there was no point hiding the fact any longer. I pulled my radio out as I ran out into the street and called the station.

"Four-three to Whisky Bravo, over!" I shouted into the radio urgently. The two men were walking quickly up the street out of the town, they looked around and saw me following fifty yards behind and broke into a run.

The station called back. I relayed the details and their direction as I chased after the men, dodging pedestrians, and they vanished around a corner. I was hoping desperately that the station would realise what I was talking about. They did and Joe said he would head for the area in a car as he was in the vicinity. I chased the men towards a car park. They jumped into a gold-coloured estate car and screeched out of the car park, I stopped, breathless, and informed Joe over the radio with the registration number and ran as fast as I could up the road to at least see which way the car went. I was sure now this was the same two men! The earlier incidents had mentioned a similar car.

A minute later Joe radioed that he had stopped the car, the two men were arrested and taken to the station. I was pleased with the result. I had once again shown how effective I could be. It was later commented on by Sgt Lakin. The incident served to boost my flagging morale.

It needed a boost. Only a few weeks earlier my whole life was sorting itself out, now I did not know where I stood. The only certain thing was that I could not walk out of the specials, it was too big a part of my life. I only hoped that I might be able to sort something out later; or that I would be successful with another force. And then there was Mike.

Since we first met in March, we saw each other regularly. We were getting on very well; we were good friends. Yet I was beginning to realise that there was a problem. I did not feel anything deeper; we were just particularly good friends. All my energy was being channelled into my police work.

A pleasant diversion was the annual party I organised every summer for all the friends in the caving group. At least I still had all my friends there. But as it turned out, my problems were only just beginning.

The party went very well, everyone was having a fun time, and several people were getting very drunk. As usual, there was an open invitation for anyone who had too much to drink to stop overnight, and several people would. I was pleased to see Sharon and Colin again; they had recently returned from Germany where Colin was stationed, and I had missed them.

Then, as the party died down and was ending in the early hours of the morning, Sharon's brother, John, decided it was time he left. He tried to get out of the chair but slumped back. He was helped up and staggered towards the front door. I had been watching him throughout the evening, he had drunk two or three glasses of Sharon's famous and strong punch before sharing a full bottle of Whisky with Phil. The bottle was now empty, and Sharon's brother was extremely drunk. After climbing into his van, against the advice of everyone there, someone grabbed his keys and brought them to me. I hid them in the house. John got out of his van and became very abusive, demanding his keys back and staggered back towards the house. The tension was building, Sharon was not around to pacify him; she and Colin had left earlier in a taxi.

There was absolutely no way I was going to give John the keys until he was sober, yet he became insistent he was going to drive back to Stafford. He lunged towards me, hatred in his expression. Several hands grabbed and restrained him. He would not listen to reason; I had no choice. He struggled and became violent, struggling aggressively to get free, the furniture was in danger of being damaged. I phoned the police station. Someone else phoned Sharon and suggested she get back around.

A couple of minutes later a police car pulled up and Sgt Dave Jones and a special walked into the mayhem. It did the trick, John calmed down yet still insisted he wanted the keys back. Sharon and Colin walked back in; Sharon glared at me. What had I done wrong? Eventually, Sharon and Colin took John and his keys back to their house. Early the next morning the van was gone. There was no way that John would have been sober even by that time.

Suddenly, the conflict that Inspector Cooper had warned me about all those years before, was rammed home. I was the culprit; it had been my fault. Suddenly neither Sharon nor Colin wanted to know me, and very rapidly I lost most of the friends I had built up over the years before joining the police. Now even more than before, my police work was my whole life. I re-doubled my efforts to get somewhere in the police service, and I continued regular duties not knowing what else I could do.

Meanwhile, officers I knew in the force were trying to find out why I had been rejected for my application to the regulars and obscenely and baffling, not having a paid job being used as the reason. I waited, hoping it could be sorted out. As the summer slipped into autumn and then to winter, I began socialising much more with Steve Smith and one or two of the other officers from the station. I put the caving group and my former friends behind me.

A gradual realisation that despite the efforts and commitment that I had given to Staffordshire Police had got me nowhere led to a decision to look elsewhere. I wrote for and returned an application form to West Midlands Police.

In the meantime, whilst I was waiting, I continued working regularly at the station. 1990 proved to be a busy year. One Saturday afternoon in April we were diverted to a report of a road accident on the A51 between Lichfield and Rugeley. We were the first patrol there and it proved to be much worse than we had expected. Two cars had collided head-on at high speed. A young man aged 19 who had been thrown from the vehicle travelling from Rugeley was lying on the roadside. Despite the efforts of a passing nurse to revive him, he died with me holding his hand. A middle-aged woman was trapped in the other car, seriously injured but semi-conscious. The door was damaged, and we couldn't force it open to get to her. She was only released when the fire and rescue cut the roof off the car. She died before reaching the hospital. I took a roadside statement from a shocked but relieved couple who had been travelling towards Lichfield when a car had overtaken them at high speed before spinning out of control into the car travelling towards them. It later turned out that the youth had been drinking in Rugeley before setting off for Lichfield. He was drunk. As a direct result, he had not only killed himself but also a woman travelling from Lichfield to visit friends in Rugeley. I was more certain than ever that I had done the right thing at what turned out to be the last of my parties.

My spirits were lifted when my section officer told me that the station had received a letter from West Midlands Police requesting a report about my work in the specials. The force would send a report back to West Midlands and hopefully, I would soon get an interview.

A Tuesday night in early May turned out to be one of the most unbelievable incidents I had ever dealt with. In the early hours of the morning, on duty without incident, we were diverted to a side road near the town centre, where two men had been seen breaking into a van parked on a street just beyond the town centre car parks and service areas. A minute later all the patrols converged on the area.

Jeff had beaten us to it by a few seconds, he was running down towards a narrow hump-backed canal bridge; he had seen someone. We jumped out of the car and ran after him; he was chasing someone. He stopped on the bridge and there was a loud splash – someone had fallen or jumped into the canal. Sure enough, as I peered over the bridge a shadowy figure was splashing around in the middle of the cut. Very soon several officers were peering down at the guy in the canal, our torches trained on him like spotlights.

"Come on, you might as well get out now!" said Jeff, hopefully.

The guy didn't reply but instead began swimming straight down the middle of the canal, under the bridge, serenely doing breaststrokes. We ran around to the towpath on the far side of the bridge, following him, but despite our protestations, he was not going to come out. We set off at a slow walk down the towpath begging him to come to the bank, he was deaf to our entreaties, continuing his sedate breaststroke. Someone was going to have to get in to pull him out, but no one volunteered.

Suddenly, we realised what he was up to. On the far side of the canal was a high brick wall, an old mill building with a towering brick wall straight into the canal, but just a few yards beyond that, residential back gardens led straight down to the canal...

"Steve! Run around to the gardens and catch him!" shouted Sgt Lakin.

Without a second's hesitation, I ran back up the towpath,

over the bridge and down Mill Lane, past the van with its open back door and tools strewn about, until I reached the first house. Where was he now? Damn it! My radio was not working, and I had to resort to shouting. I could hear the other bobbies on the far bank, beyond the houses.

Scrambling over hedges and fences I soon found myself in a small, neat back garden. I could see all my colleagues lined up on the opposite bank of the canal beyond the garden, their torches trained on the bank of the garden I was in.

"He's in there Steve!" shouted Jeff.

I looked around, shining my torch everywhere around the garden but, there was no sign of anyone. Frantically I ran around the garden, peering between rosebushes and the shrubbery around the ornamental pond, then searched again. Lights were coming on in the houses around and faces appeared at windows. A window opened in the house above me, and a face peered out. I shone the torch on my uniform,

"It's OK, sir, it's the police, we're looking for someone who's just climbed into your garden from the canal."

"Try the garage, the door isn't locked." said the man, pointing to the corner of the house below him. I ran over to the doorway, making a mental note to send around the crime prevention officer at some point!

Opening the garage door, I stepped cautiously inside, this was the only place left for the elusive thief. I looked under the car. But it was not the place where the soaking-wet thief was, no one was in the garage. I walked back out into the garden, puzzled and frustrated.

"He's not here!" I shouted back to my colleagues still waiting on the far bank.

"He is! We saw him get out of the canal there, he's got to be there somewhere!"

I ran frantically around the garden again, certain that he must have escaped into a neighbouring garden in the confusion.

I was joined in the garden by Andy, who had recently transferred to Rugeley from Cannock. For most of the evening so far, he had been holed up in an industrial unit nearby as part of an operation to catch the gang responsible for a spate of burglaries there. He was eager to join us, thankful for the break! Together we searched, but to no avail. I had been in the garden for at least five minutes now, but apart from me and Andy, there was no one else there.

I made one last effort, shining my torch under every shrub and bush and then, as it trailed across the surface of the ornamental pond, I noticed a tiny ripple. Sure enough, in the corner of the pond, a nose had just broken surface before going under again. No, it was not possible! The pond was only five or six feet long – but as I trained my torch beam on the water, I could make out the dim outline of a figure under the surface. Andy joined me.

"OK, you might as well come out now!" I said loudly, pointing the torch beam at the face.

A filthy, slime-covered, and extremely smelly figure appeared, dripping, from the surface of the pond. I really hoped he would come quietly; I didn't fancy struggling with him. Yet as we reached out to grab him, his muscles tensed as he made another attempt to evade arrest. He lunged towards the canal, and I had no choice but to commit myself to rugby tackle him to the ground. Squelch! He was like a giant, slimy, extremely smelly slug.

Jeff came around and joined us in the garden. Together the three of us were having great difficulty restraining the man, he was struggling violently and was extremely slimy and slippery. We were all sliding slowly but perilously across the lawn towards the canal bank. Despite my best efforts, we were only feet away from sliding into the canal. No way! We dragged him back up the garden, but he was still struggling violently. It did not matter by this time; I was filthy now anyway. I managed to get one-half of my handcuff onto one of his wrists, but he then dragged that arm underneath him, taking the flailing empty handcuff with him. Dangerous! We could not pull his arm out; it was a potentially dangerous time, if he swung his cuffed arm about with that handcuff swinging from it, he could seriously injure one of us. Despite tugging he would not give in, his arm remained fixed underneath him. Eventually, after a further almighty struggle, we got his arm out and got the other handcuff onto his free wrist. We lay for a few seconds, all panting, then hauled him up and led him out of the garden, to cheers from the spectators above. What a show for them!

Throughout all this, the man was never violent towards any officer, just absolutely determined to evade arrest, yet he had only been arrested for a relatively minor offence. I had never known anyone to put so much effort into just 'getting away!'

I returned to the station, exhausted and out of breath but proud of my achievement…only to be turned back at the door of the control room by Jan, the controller.

"Get out you smelly animal! You're not coming in here like that, Johnson!"

I got a lift home from a reluctant officer, had a shower, and changed, half an hour later I was back at the station in a fresh uniform and a lot cleaner.

And so, I continued to work throughout 1990, putting in even more hours as other shifts were stretched to the limit when officers were taken off to work on squads after several terrorist incidents over the Midlands.

I waited for a reply from West Midlands police, but nothing was forthcoming. Despite a phone enquiry, I heard no more. Yet they had received the application, and they had contacted headquarters for a report. Somewhere along the line, my application hit a brick wall and I was beginning to realise that neither would I get anywhere with the West Midlands Police.

As the year passed and 1991 approached, I saw less and less of Mike. I was heading up a blind alley once again, my plan to change my life had ground to a halt. I was working hard in the specials, but it was getting me nowhere, I had lost direction. As 1991 progressed I had one diversion to look forward to at least. My parents were paying for me to go on holiday with them to Switzerland, and I became even more excited as the date approached. I have loved mountains all my life and the Alps had been an ambition of mine for a long time.

Despite feeling exhausted after the number of hours I had been working with no real break and the way I had been swapping and changing my duties to accommodate the shortcomings on various shifts, my energy was renewed just by the thought of the imminent holiday. Nevertheless, I desperately needed a break. One night towards the end of August I hardly slept, we had to get up at three-thirty to get to the airport on time. Within a few hours, we had landed at Zurich and were travelling by coach into the heart of the Alps.

After we passed Bern, the tiny capital, the landscape became wilder, and peering ahead I could see the mountains rising ever higher. After appearing from a tunnel next to Lake Thün the mountains towered over us. After a brief stop in Interlaken to drop off passengers we were heading up the Lauterbrünnen

Valley. Cliffs rose precipitously above the pine forests to great heights on either side of the narrow gorge before suddenly opening out into one of the most breathtaking sights I had ever seen as we entered Lauterbrünnen.

The Valley opened out beyond the village and on either side, immense vertical cliffs rose several thousand feet and above them towered the glistening flanks of the Oberland giants, the Eiger, the Mönch and the Jungfrau, its summit was more than ten thousand feet above us. Tolkien had visited the valley in his youth and it had made an equally powerful impression on him as it was the Latuerbrünnen Valley which was his model for Rivendell in his The Lord of the Rings trilogy.

The journey up to Mürren was hardly less spectacular. A funicular straight up the impossibly steep mountainside to a small station several thousand feet above and then a short train journey through meadows with this incredible backdrop to the village of Mürren, perched high on the edge of the cliff overlooking the awesome ice cliffs and peaks opposite. Our hotel perched precariously on the edge of the cliff had a grandstand view of the incredible scenery around us.

The holiday was wonderful, Switzerland was everything that the clichés made it. Cowbells, yodelling choirs, alpenhorns, and incredibly efficient public transport. We walked up and down mountain tracks, walked on glaciers and enjoyed the warm sun and clear, fresh mountain air. I returned home two weeks later, sad to be leaving, determined to get back as soon as possible, thoroughly refreshed. And to a phone call from Mike.

Mike very apologetically explained that he had met someone else and that he was calling off what was left of any relationship we had ever had.

I was relieved, it had been bothering me for a long time. I

knew we were getting nowhere together; I was pleased for him. He came over for a day or two soon after and ironically, with the tension gone, we enjoyed each other's company more than we had for a long time.

With nothing better to do, I was back on duty within a few days. In between duties, I spent time working on some large pen and ink drawings. My creative energy had been renewed by the holiday and I was keen to convey the memories of my experience of the Alps. I began a drawing of the mighty Aletsch Glacier which we had walked on, over eleven thousand feet above sea level. The sight of the incredible frozen river of ice – the largest and longest glacier in Europe, stretching far into the distance, was overwhelming and still strong in my memory.

After finishing that, I began another drawing, this time of the Eiger viewed from above the village of Grindelwald, the towering, dark and forbidding North face, an incredible, almost vertical, convex wall of rock a mile high, one of the most difficult climbs in the world and notorious for the number of climbers killed whilst attempting it. We had visited the Grindelwald glacier above the village while on holiday, and there was an intense thunderstorm while we were there. As we headed down towards Grindelwald village again after the storm, the shredding clouds opened views of the Eiger summit high above, and as the clouds cleared rays of sunlight lit up the North face which had made a similar haunting impression in my mind and which I had to convey on paper. I couldn't finish this drawing, I put it to one side, half-finished; it was proving exceedingly difficult, although I did eventually finish it.

In between drawing sessions, I spent my time on duty or in the Prince of Wales with Steve Smith or some of the other officers. I was becoming frustrated by my lack of progress, which heightened since Mike, and I had split up. Increasingly frequently our conversations in the pub would turn to my frustration.

"What's up, mate?"

"Oh, nothing much Steve. I'm just getting a bit fed up, I'm not getting anywhere, you know…"

I stared thoughtfully at the dried foam patterns on the inside of my glass.

"What are you fed up with?"

I thought about it. Job, but mostly lack of a partner. But I could not tell him that.

"Oh, you know, just…things. Nothing. It doesn't matter."

We sat staring at our rapidly emptying glasses again. Steve was going to probe further in a minute, and I was going to have to lie to him, which I did not like doing, or change the subject quickly. I looked up at Steve.

"Do you fancy another pint?"

"Yes, I'll have another."

I got up and walked to the bar, relieved but frustrated. I needed to talk to someone, but not Steve, he would not understand. How would he take the fact that I was gay?

Steve knew something was wrong, but there was nothing I could say to him, I became increasingly anxious that my life had stagnated, something had to happen to change it. I had to meet someone else – but how? And I had to sort my career out. I was getting nowhere with the police service, despite the record I had. It just did not make any sense.

A career in the police was out of the question. Yet I also realised it had become my whole life, I could not just abandon it. Whichever way my life went, whatever career I ended up in, I would not, could not give up my position in the specials. At least now, I knew where I stood there. And so, as 1991 ended, I split my time between drawing, drinks in the pub and duties.

Christmas 1991 proved to be eventful, at least concerning my police duties. Christmas day was, surprisingly, remarkably busy. My shift was working earlies for the second year running, but I quite enjoyed working earlies on Christmas Day. Christmas Day the year before had been a quiet, festive, and hugely enjoyable duty. But before I finished at two this year, I attended a serious road accident and two unrelated house fires, one of them a major fire. Although no one was seriously hurt in any of the incidents, I couldn't imagine the upset to those families on Christmas day.

I was earning enough in expenses because of the number of hours I was working, to consider another holiday in Switzerland. My cousin Robert was interested, we had spent a lot of time walking and caving together over the years, so early in January, I booked two weeks at the Alpina Hotel in Mürren for us both, something I could eagerly look forward to. Yet it was still bothering me. Really, I would rather have been going to Switzerland with a partner. A solution suggested itself to me one day, when I noticed, whilst idly leafing through one of the local free papers, that they had started a page of personal ads. I scanned through them and was surprised but excited to see that a few of them were from gay men. I decided at once that I would use these columns to help me find a partner.

I went back on duty much more optimistic that 1992 would be a bit more positive for me than the one that just ended. From then on, I waited eagerly every week for the paper to drop through the letterbox and, when no one was looking, I scanned through the ads for any that looked interesting. I began sending letters to some and even placed one myself in the hope that at last, I might meet someone. At least these were from people living locally. I began to correspond with other gay people from the area. But, frustratingly, no one was special, so I had to keep trying. I was determined not to give up.

As the months passed by, I still had not met anyone special. Yet I was not too bothered. The nearer the summer got; the closer Switzerland was getting again. I was already getting excited. Robert and I decided to spend some time together walking before going to Switzerland so that Robert could get fit enough for some of the Alpine treks. We spent a wonderful week camping near Lyme Regis in Dorset and spent a lot of it walking.

Soon after returning home the following week, Brian from Stafford contacted me, from an advertisement I had answered in the paper. We talked on the phone for quite a while and seemed to get on. We arranged to meet in Rugeley one Saturday afternoon a week or two later. I met Brian in the Prince of Wales car park as planned; it was a hot, cloudless June day. We set off walking across the fields towards Cannock Chase, talking and joking. But the further we got away from the town the clearer it became that Brian only wanted one thing – sex. It turned out that he was married and had a child, he was not in a position or had any inclination to have any form of relationship. I did not find him particularly attractive and was completely put off by his suggestions. I was eager to return to civilisation. When I left him in the car park an hour later, I was relieved yet frustrated that once again I had not found a way through or over this high and impregnable brick wall in my life.

I walked back home dispirited and fed up. There was a note on the window ledge in my room in my mother's hand. Somebody called Paul had phoned me whilst I had been out. A phone number was left with a message saying he would call later that evening. Paul was one of the ads I had sent a letter to a week earlier.

I ran to the phone when it rang later that evening, with a sense of excitement and curiosity.

"Hello?"

"Is that Steve?"

"Yes, it is."

"It's Paul here. I phoned earlier and spoke to your mother, I think. You sent me a letter a week or so ago."

"Yes, that's right! Hello Paul, how are you!"

Two hours later I replaced the handset. Paul and I had so much in common! We got on extremely well and I could have talked for hours, he was so easy to get on with. Paul also lived with his parents; he had not yet told them he was gay. We both liked the sound of each other and agreed to talk again very soon. Even better, he lived just a few minutes away across Cannock Chase. The following day we had a further phone conversation for a couple of hours. It was time Paul and I met. As had happened just recently, I agreed to meet him in the car park of the Prince of Wales one evening a few days later, I just hoped that it would be a better experience than last time.

I walked down to the car park nervous and excited, hoping that our meeting would be as interesting as our phone conversations had been. Hoping that he would be there – I had been let down in the past by people I was supposed to be meeting. But his car was parked in the car park, and I walked nervously towards it. Paul got out. He was tall, slim, blond, and good-looking. We exchanged greetings and walked into the pub. Hours later, after we'd had a lengthy conversation, we left and Paul drove me home, calling in for a coffee. He left for home an hour or two later, agreeing to meet again very soon.

I walked back into the house excited and elated. For the first time in my life, I had found someone else who was gay and whom I could relate to, talk to, and like very much. I knew that my life was about to change at last, but I had no idea by just how much, in what direction or exactly how, and perhaps it was best that I didn't know.

I met Paul again a week later and again we talked for hours. I was certain that at the very least we were going to become particularly good friends. There was nothing about which we could not talk. For the first time in my life, I began to discuss my sexuality with another person. Never had I ever felt comfortable using the word *gay* or *homosexual*. I could talk about being gay for the first time without feeling embarrassed.

Yet I was worried when Paul told me that since meeting me, he had met Gary who had also replied to the same advertisement. I hoped that our friendship would last and that Paul would not suddenly lose interest in me for Gary. I needed to be able to trust Paul. In the end, I had to voice my concern and Paul reassured me that whatever happened in the future we would remain friends. I felt more positive, more in control of my life at last than I had for a long time. We began to meet regularly, and every time Paul left, I longed for the next time I would see him, I felt closer to Paul than I had to anyone before.

I approached my police duties with a new sense of optimism. I returned to the station full of energy, incredibly positive and looking forward, at last to the future. Out on foot patrol, late one evening with Kevin, we passed a drunk man slumped on a bench in the town centre. We stopped and spoke to him, but he said he would make his way home. He was not abusive or violent, so we left him to sort himself out and make his way home, and continued our patrol, chatting.

At about midnight Ian Gilbey, who was now the shift

controller, diverted the other patrol car to a burglary in progress. I looked across to Kev and nodded – we were close on foot to the location, so he called the station and said we would make the area in case they wanted any help. To our surprise, Ian called back to say no, he did not want us to go there, but could we instead return to the station straight away? I looked at Kev, puzzled. It did not seem right, what on earth could override our need to assist with a possible burglary? A minute or two later we were crossing the street to the forecourt in front of the station.

As we walked towards the front door, I noticed a pile of freshly broken glass near the gate post and as we stepped through the swing doors into the tiny foyer, we realised soon enough the reason for Ian's strange request and the broken glass. The drunk we had seen earlier in the town centre was standing in the foyer.

The place reeked of stale alcohol. Ian was standing behind the glass screen, perfectly safe. As we entered Ian shouted to the drunk through the partition.

"Put that bottle down!"

The drunk held the broken neck, the remains of the whisky bottle he had just smashed on the gate post, waving it around, using the neck as a handle, the jagged broken end pointed menacingly towards us. It was now clear why Ian had wanted us to return to the station so quickly. I backed against the far wall; Kev stepped back towards the entrance. I was scared. This was dangerous.

"What's the problem?" asked Kev, as calmly as he could.

"You don't understand." said the drunk, his speech slurred.

Ian had vacated the hatch and slowly and carefully opened the door from the station, just behind me, and joined us in the foyer. All the time the jagged broken end of the bottle was waved menacingly, only a couple of feet away by the very drunk man.

"What's it all about Ian?" Kev asked quietly and calmly.

"The gentleman seems to think he is owed some money, and he wants *us* to do something about it," replied Ian, with his usual dry sarcasm.

"Put the bottle down, mate," Kev asked calmly, "and We'll try and sort out what your problem is".

"Fuck off!" was the reply, and to prove he meant it, the bottle hovered even closer. I backed off. My right hand slipped unobserved down to the strap of my truncheon, slowly I slipped my thumb through the loop, eased it out and held it behind my back. I had come close to it but never needed to use it in anger before now.

"Come on, first put that bottle down, then let's talk about it," Kev asked again.

"Fuck off!"

It would only have taken a couple of seconds for the three of us to overpower the man, but in that time, he could have seriously injured or maimed any one of us with a glancing blow from the razor edge of the bottle. And he was in a volatile enough state to use it. We each knew we had to wait for exactly the right moment, but in the meantime, extreme caution and tact were needed to keep the man as calm as possible. I tried talking to the man.

"What's your name, mate?"

"Fuck off!"

"What's your first name, we only want to help you."

"Fuck off! What's *your* name?"

"Steve."

"Well fuck off Steve, I'm leaving."

"No, you're not, we can't let you go outside as upset as you are, put that bottle down first and let's talk about it sensibly," I replied, just slightly more forcefully.

The man backed towards the door. There was absolutely no way we could let him out in the state he was, with the broken bottle and in the mood that he was in. Kev stepped back against the entrance and held the doors shut, blocking any exit.

"Look, please just put that bottle down!" asked Kev.

"I'm leaving now! Move, or else...!"

The man turned towards Kev, glaring, and waving the bottle close to Kev's face. Kev backed off and I stepped forward, just in case, bringing my truncheon around ready to use.

"I'm not moving." said Kev calmly and deliberately, "Put that bottle down."

"There's only one way I'm going. Out there..." said the man, waving the bottle towards the entrance, "...or up there."

He put the broken edge of the bottle against his own throat.

"Stop being silly..." I said, "We really can sort this out if you calm down and let us help you."

The man slowly lowered the bottle from his throat, glaring at me. This was our opportunity, but we had to be quick and decisive. There would be no retake or second chance!

Simultaneously we both lunged for the arm holding the bottle and grabbed it firmly. The man struggled violently, but there was no way I was going to lose my grip on his arm. Ian put his arm around the man's neck and between us, we pulled him to the ground. I pulled backwards on the arm until his grip relented and the bottle dropped, to my relief, onto the floor, smashing some more, shards flying around. I managed to kick the main part of it out of reach, to the far side of the narrow foyer. Kev took immense pleasure in telling the man that he was now under arrest. We managed, with a great deal of struggling, to drag the man into the station.

There appeared to be no plain reason for his behaviour, it

just seemed to prove, once again, just how unpredictable, and violent some people can get when they get drunk. When I later told Paul about what had happened, he was concerned for my safety. He considered police work to be extremely dangerous and suggested I should consider giving it up. There was no way I was going to do that, but it was touching that he was so genuinely worried about me, he cared about me.

There were other matters on my mind now. Switzerland was only weeks away; I was getting quite excited. I saw my cousin Rob several times in preparation. In the meantime, I saw Paul once or twice a week and we spoke on the phone every evening. Whenever Paul dropped me at home, we would linger in the car talking for several minutes, and then, before leaving Paul would lean across, after checking that no one could see, and we kissed. Nothing heavy, just a sign of genuine care and, dare I think it, even love between us.

Suddenly Switzerland was only a day or two away. The excitement was growing, and I began to pack my case. I only had one concern about the holiday. I had never told Rob, my cousin, that I was gay. I was worried that he might see the holiday as an opportunity to pick up girls, I had no idea how I would deal with any suggestions like that.

As it turned out, there were no problems at all. Switzerland was every bit as wonderful as I had remembered. We got drunk, and we walked up mountains and along forest trails for miles. One day we walked up to Almendhübel, a grassy clearing about an hour's walk above the village with stunning views of the Oberland mountains, and spent the entire day soaking up the sun and the local brew at a folk festival there. Before we knew it, it was the final day and night of the holiday, Swiss National Day, August 1. There were parades and parties and in the evening fireworks, a fitting climax to the holiday. It had been brilliant, and yet...I was missing Paul. In some ways, I was not as disappointed as I thought I might be when the holiday ended after two weeks, and we said goodbye to Cecile and Werner Taugwalder.

I was soon back at the station and on duty. I still worked primarily with shift two. There had been several changes to the shift since I had joined five years earlier, Sgt Lakin had moved sometime before and Dave had transferred to the CID in Cannock, much to my disappointment, a couple of years earlier. Since then, he had left the police altogether. He was now self-employed living a few miles north of Rugeley. I had not seen him for a year or so, it was about time we met up for a drink, I decided.

I phoned him one evening soon after returning from Switzerland. We agreed to meet at a pub halfway between Rugeley and his house the following week. He had something important to tell me, but it would have to wait until we met. I was intrigued and could not imagine what news he had that was so important to me. Paul came along when I went out to see Dave. I was proud to have Paul with me, although Dave would not know about us. I was looking forward to seeing Dave again, he had been a good mate to me, I had learnt a lot about policing from him and I missed working with him. Besides that, I was intrigued to find out what it was he had to tell me. As it turned out, what Dave did tell me answered a few questions which had been frustrating and puzzling me for a long time. Dave had been reliably informed, by an ex-colleague, that my former friend Toby had known, a week before I went, that I would be turned down at my interview at headquarters to join the regulars. Therefore, it was a foregone conclusion. The real reason, I finally realised, was because I was gay, which Toby knew, and of course that had become a problem for him. It was a shock. As we left the pub and said goodbye to Dave, I knew that he had not realised exactly *what* he had just told me, merely that Toby knew I would not get in. Yet it was blatantly obvious to me now what the issue was.

It had been staring me in the face for all these years! Many people, some very senior colleagues included, had expressed their concern and surprise that I had been rejected for the regular force. They said, as I too realised, that Staffordshire Police's reason for rejecting me was an excuse, it was not the real reason I was rejected. Yet no one could find the underlying cause of it. It all made sense now. Toby had not wanted anyone to know we were friends when I joined the specials because at that time he alone knew I was gay. What did he tell them at headquarters? I always knew they were hiding the real reason and now I realised what it was. It could only be one thing, it made perfect sense, but I knew I could never prove it.

Chapter 6

Opening Doors

I was relieved, at least, that my rejected application to the regulars, which had puzzled me for so long, now seemed to make perfect sense. It also made sense of the way my application to West Midlands Police had hit the same brick wall when they contacted Stafford. There was no way I would get into the regular force now that they knew I was gay. But what did it matter now? I had already accepted that a police career was obviously out of the question sometime before, even though I did not know what barrier I was up against. I had already resigned myself to the fact that any police career would remain in the specials. Once again Paul suggested I should consider leaving the police. But why should I? I enjoyed the work! Yet I was aware, even at this stage, that my life was, at last, moving on at a rapidly increasing pace. Even more to the point, I was changing.

Over the following few weeks, the pattern of my life slowly but inexorably altered and colleagues at the station were noticing. I did not drink with Steve Smith quite so often because some nights I would see Paul instead. Then, when I worked the afternoon shift, instead of working right through until ten I would, very occasionally, book the last hour or two off and finish at seven or eight if I had arranged to see Paul. And I began encouraging him to meet me from the station. It was a dare, a risk I was enjoying. I almost wanted them to know. I wanted them to know how I felt towards Paul. My whole attitude to my sexuality had changed, I was becoming much more confident.

One evening Paul picked me up from the station and we went around to the Prince of Wales for a drink. The conversation turned to gay clubs and bars and Paul suggested we should try one sometime soon. Neither of us had ever been anywhere near a gay club before. I was quite worried. What would they be like? I imagined it to be a seedy, twilight world of sex, drugs and loud music. I changed the subject.

The next time I saw Paul, he told me that he knew where there was a gay club called The Nightingale in Birmingham. After a lot of persuading, I agreed to go.

"Why are you finishing so early tomorrow night?" asked Kev when I told the sergeant I would be finishing at seven.

"I'm going out for the evening with a friend," I replied, not lying, but neither telling the whole truth.

The following day Paul arrived mid-evening to pick me up. We drove over to Birmingham and parked in a side street near the city centre, Paul had previously checked out where the entrance of the club was. I was nervous but very curious. My pulse quickened as we walked into Thorp Street. I looked around, quite a few people were walking along the street, but how many of them were gay, how many were heading for the Nightingale?

There was a 'straight' pub opposite the Nightingale where we were going to have a drink first. We walked into the pub, ordered a pint each and found a table near the window. I sipped my pint, curiously watching the people walking along the street outside. They seemed quite ordinary. Paul discreetly pointed out the entrance of the club, opposite. It was a plain, non-descript door in an otherwise plain brick wall.

I watched and soon saw a middle-aged man enter the club.

A minute later a couple of younger blokes followed him in. This was interesting, I had never knowingly seen gay people walking about in public before, not with any certainty. I knew I must have, but now I knew for certain. I glanced nervously at my watch. Paul had finished his pint and I finished mine.

"Shall we go?" Paul asked.

"OK, I'm ready."

We walked out of the pub. My pulse was racing, and my mind was concentrating on the doorway opposite. Walking quickly across the road, conscious that anyone who saw me now might know I was gay, I followed Paul into the club.

I was relieved as the door closed behind me. The sound of loud, amplified music came from a room further in. After paying our entrance fee I followed Paul through into the bar. Two or three dozen other men were standing around in groups, as couples or singly. I was conscious of several pairs of eyes looking at me as I followed Paul to the bar. Again, we ordered drinks and found a convenient place to one side. So, these were all gay men. I had never seen so many together before, and I was fascinated. The atmosphere was much more relaxed than the tense state I had worked myself into. Some of the men were quite obviously camp and effeminate but many others were very ordinary-looking guys, I would never have guessed that they were gay if I had passed them in the street. But then again, would anybody know I was?

I was very conscious that everybody in the club would know I was gay; this was something which I had never really experienced before. Yes, I had told some of my close friends several years earlier, but this was different. These were strangers. Damn it! What did it matter anyway? These men were all gay themselves, so why should I be bothered? I relaxed and began to enjoy the atmosphere. From that moment on my whole outlook changed. In complete contrast, I began to enjoy the sensation that these strangers would look at me and know that I was gay. Instead of hiding and being ashamed, I became almost proud. Why proud? It was a natural reaction against a society which told me I should be ashamed to be gay which for the first time I had just started to experience. Why should I feel ashamed? I couldn't help being gay, it is just the way I turned out! The difference in my outlook was profound.

I walked out of the Nightingale an hour later a different person. I enjoyed the experience. Just being in the company of other gay people had liberated me, I felt completely different. Paul picked up copies of a free gay weekly paper, *The Pink Paper* as we left. He passed one to me which I folded discreetly as we walked back to the car. Once home I leafed through it, taking in and learning about gay issues, and finding out about other gay venues. I hid it in my bedroom, out of sight of my parents, and read it from cover to cover when I knew I was on my own and my parents were not around. I looked forward to our next visit to the Nightingale a few days later.

I was still nervous as we walked into the club, but once inside I lost all that and I quickly relaxed into the atmosphere of the place. This time, feeling much more confident, we probed deeper into the club and began to explore; the noise was deafening and there were many more men of all ages in there. Once again, I felt that sense of liberation, I enjoyed displaying merely by my presence, that I was gay. But away from the club, once back at the station, I again withdrew into my protective shell. I was beginning to lead a peculiar double life.

The shift was becoming ever more curious about where I was going, I just said I was going out to a club with a friend, which was not a lie.

One evening soon after, Paul came over with Gary. I was still unsure about Gary, to me he was a potential threat to the friendship I now had with Paul. Yet we got on quite well, although I sensed that Gary was also very wary of me, for the same reason. On the next visit to the Nightingale club, all three of us went. It was better going as part of a small group; I was enjoying the atmosphere. We began going out to the cinema regularly. Together with our forays into Birmingham and evenings in the Prince of Wales, I was now seeing Paul at least two or three times a week. Yet we were not getting bored with each other's company. Our conversations never dried up.

One evening Paul mentioned a gay club he had seen advertised in the Pink Paper called Gavans in Wolverhampton. We decided to try it out soon instead of driving into Birmingham.

Gavan's was slightly nearer than the Nightingale, so it might be a better place to go. The following Saturday evening Paul picked me up then drove over to Gary's and picked him up before setting off for Wolverhampton. Paul knew where to park; he had looked for the club one afternoon while driving through Wolverhampton. After parking on a side street, we set off for the club. Unlike Birmingham, there was a line of people queueing to get in. But it did not bother me now, I did not mind the possibility of people seeing me and knowing that by being in the queue I was probably gay.

The club was completely different from The Nightingale. We wandered onto a huge dance floor, there was a bar at the far end. We set off to explore. Alcoves with seating and tables lined the edges of the room and beyond the bar was a snack bar with tables and seats. A balcony ran around the hall upstairs with seats and tables and there was a separate bar area.

After buying drinks we found a quiet alcove to sit and watch as more people of all descriptions filed in. By mid-evening the club was becoming quite busy, the vast empty spaces rapidly filling with happy, smiling, laughing people of all ages and types. And yet still they filed in. As eleven approached the club was heaving with people, but still, they came in; there must have been upwards of a thousand people in the club, it was amazing! I could never have imagined seeing so many gay people together in one place.

At eleven the show started after a dramatic musical build-up, the music boomed out and the lights began dancing, the atmosphere was wild, intoxicating. It was difficult to talk on the main dance floor, we wandered around looking for a quieter corner to chat. Then we wandered back into the main hall, mingling with the crowds around the edge of the seething, bobbing mass a few feet further onto the dance floor. Gary followed Paul into the crowd, pushing their way into the middle of the dance floor. I watched for a couple of minutes before following them on. Three hours later we staggered out of the club into the quiet, cool early morning air, my ears were ringing. If the Nightingale had liberated me, Gavan's had just propelled me forwards into a state of near euphoria, never again would I feel embarrassment or shame about my sexuality!

Paul dropped me at home, with my latest copy of the Pink Paper an hour or so later after dropping Gary off. Over a cup of tea, I leafed through the paper before hiding it and going to bed. From now on we began to visit Gavans in preference to the Nightingale on about every Saturday night and the occasional night in between. In between, I put in regular duties with my shift at the station. I was aware that my situation there was getting slightly awkward, my drastic lifestyle change had been noticed, and my change in mood was commented on.

One afternoon whilst I was in the parade room with Kev and the shift sergeant, the phone rang. Kev answered it, looked across at me and surprisingly, told me it was for me, passing the receiver over to me. It was Paul. I could not hide my embarrassment as Paul, realising the situation I was in and how embarrassed I would be, made a suggestive comment and said he loved me before hanging up. I knew no one could hear anything, but this was the closest the two halves of my life had come to colliding head-on. The distance and potential conflict between my two contradictory and opposing lifestyles became ever clearer as the weeks went by. As far as possible, when questioned, I told the truth. I did not hide the fact that I was visiting a large nightclub in Wolverhampton with friends on most Saturday evenings, I just did not say what type of club.

I was not surprised by my colleague's curiosity as I had worked constantly and closely with them for a long time, some for several years. Some were good friends. As the weeks went by it slowly dawned on me that eventually some at least would find out soon even if I said nothing.

And they were getting closer to the truth. Then the ribbing started. Who was she? What was her name? Where did I meet her? It was becoming unbearably difficult to lie to my friends and I didn't want to, and the ribbing was becoming relentless. Besides, I was becoming ever more confident about my sexuality; the euphoria, the exhilaration of suddenly discovering myself, was overwhelming. I almost wanted to tell everyone – to stand on top of a high hill and shout as loudly as I could – but I was far too reserved for that.

One evening I went out on foot patrol with Deb, one of the female specials. She had joined a year or so earlier and ever since joining there were rumours around the station that she might be, you know, like that. I suspected as much myself but had not liked to ask.

We spent a few minutes standing in a deeply recessed shop doorway in the town centre, watching people walking by, keeping our eye on the town centre – it was a good vantage point, a favourite of mine. Using the reflections in the shop windows opposite it was possible to see quite a lot of the town centre whilst being invisible ourselves. Often people would walk right past without realising anyone was watching and listening! Sometimes we said 'Boo!' as people walked past, making them jump and we burst out laughing.

We stood and talked quietly. This was the first time I had had a good chat with Deb. Was I going out anywhere this weekend? she asked. I hesitated for several seconds before replying that I was going out to a club with some friends. I was on the verge of telling her but backed away at the last second. But I did tell her it was in Wolverhampton.

Later, at home, I thought for a long time about my predicament. Despite reservations, I was on so much of a 'high' since meeting Paul that I wanted everyone to know. Quite apart from that, I was increasingly aware that some of my colleagues and friends at the station were getting ever closer to the truth. Now they were putting two and two together and getting five. Very soon, I realised, it would be four. Knowing full well how fast rumours can spread, not just around the station, or even around the division, but right around the county, I decided it would be better if I told them the truth. Besides that, some of these colleagues were friends whom I trusted, and I felt increasingly guilty that I was not being honest with them.

Having decided, at last, that I would 'come out' to my

colleagues, I had to work out how best to carry it out. How should I do it? Should I stand up at parade one day and make an announcement? ("Hi everyone, there's something I want to tell you. I'm gay.") No. I could never do that! In the end, I decided I would tell my closest colleagues individually. I had known them for years, some since I had joined. I would speak to just one or two of my most trusted friends and colleagues first and, depending on their reaction, I would then tell others until, by the law of the canteen culture and jungle telegraph, everyone would find out. Then I would not have to hide anything. I came out in a cold sweat when I thought about the decision I had just made. Not so long ago, I was terrified of anyone in the station finding out at all, I just did not know how I would manage it. Now I was almost looking forward to it. It showed just how profound a change I had experienced.

So, as 1992 drew towards its end, I found a convenient opportunity to speak to Sarah, my section officer. To my great relief, she was not unduly shocked, she did not seem surprised at all. I was not surprised at her reaction because one of her friends was Deb. Then I spoke to Jan, a WPC on one of the other shifts who I got on very well with. Jan was great, she was supportive and understanding and she came to be a tower of strength and support for me a few months later. Somehow it was much easier to tell females, perhaps because there was no possibility of any implied 'threat' or suggestion from their point of view. My campaign was running smoothly and to plan. This was great!

Soon afterwards I found a convenient, quiet time whilst working in the control room with Ian Gilbey, and I told him. He was reserved, quiet and tactful. He was surprised, but as I suspected, not at all shocked. I was not surprised by his reaction; Ian was intelligent enough not to believe all the lies and bigoted stereotyping so often targeted at gay people.

Then, very soon after, I found time, whilst we were out on patrol together, to tell Kev. He was very understanding too, his only comment was that if I could do the job, which was all that was important, and he knew I could; my private life did not concern him at all. So far everything was going to plan, there did not appear to be any problems. I then spoke to Colin, another section officer at the station. Once again, it was not a problem. I mentally drew up a list of other officers I would talk to when I could find the time. So far, the people who knew were very trustworthy, there probably wasn't much of a risk of it spreading to anyone else, not yet at least.

I was almost enjoying telling people I was gay, it was bizarre. Yet I realised that at some point soon I was going to have to tell my parents; so far only one of my sisters knew, she had known for years. But talking to my parents, to tell them that their only son was gay, was frightening and for the moment, impossible. Sometime soon I knew I was going to have to face up to it. I also had to speak to Steve Smith.

Steve had become a particularly good friend. He was one of the most straightforward and honest people I had ever met. Since I had tutored him when he first joined the specials four years earlier, we worked together often and even more often spent evenings in the Prince of Wales. But, probably because of his straightforward, down-to-earth, working-class nature, I hesitated. So far, my plan could not have progressed better, but I was not sure how Steve would react. I knew that sooner rather than later he was going to hear it anyway, I just wanted it to be from me, I owed him that, as a friend.

On one or two occasions in the Prince, I tried to steer the conversation around again to my frustration, but it was not working, I was finding it difficult. On one occasion I sensed he was trying to tell me something, yet even then I could not bring myself to say anything so I steered the conversation away, I would try some other time.

It was now mid-October, I had known Paul for only just over three months, yet my life had already changed beyond my wildest imaginings. Paul told me, one evening, that his friends had often told him he was a catalyst, that he changed things. It certainly seemed apt in my case. I knew I was falling in love with Paul, in a way I had never experienced before.

And yet, there were things which were troubling me. I was also worried about my feelings for Paul. He was the best thing that had ever happened to me and, through meeting him I had suddenly discovered myself. Yet I was increasingly and desperately worried about his friendship with Gary. Paul's personality was captivating. He reminded me, superficially at least, of Toby. I had implicitly trusted Toby. I just hoped it was not going to happen the same way with Paul. There was nothing I could do except see how it turned out. The following week Paul spent at a hotel in Manchester, courtesy of his company, on a training course. Even though Manchester is not too far away, it seemed like he had been taken away from me, I was missing him. He phoned mid-week with reports of his explorations of the gay 'village' there. He phoned again on Friday morning; he was on his way home and was going to call in on his way through. I could not wait, wonderful!

As it turned out, by the time he left for home I was depressed. I could not put my finger on it, but something wasn't right. I was sure it had to do with Gary. I could not stand this. I phoned him a bit later in the afternoon. Paul was also upset about something; I had never known him like this. Soon after putting the phone down and getting even more upset and worried than I had been, Paul phoned back; we would go out to the cinema later! It cheered me up. Later, that evening, back at home after returning from the cinema, sitting in Paul's car on the drive, we talked and talked, it cleared the air. We hugged and kissed before he left.

Despite feeling uneasy about Paul's relationship with Gary, I was increasingly more certain that we had become too close for him to forget our friendship, even if that was all I had. I knew he cared about me. One evening a week or two later at a now customary trip to Gavan's, Paul and Gary called round to pick me up, Paul had a quiet, discreet word before we left. He and Gary were formally seeing each other. Effectively, Paul was telling me he had become engaged to Gary. I sat down, completely mixed up emotionally. I knew it was going to happen. Paul tried to reassure me that we would remain close friends, yet that evening was the loneliest and most miserable I had spent at Gavans. I could not help feeling left out as they danced, very obviously together.

I continued to see Paul just as often as I had been, yet I was still worried. Somehow, I could not forget the way Toby had treated me. I grew increasingly alarmed and worried about the situation I had gotten myself into. I still did not have a paid job and I was concerned that it might have been an influence on the way things had just gone. My whole life was the police, yet even here now I was on a rollercoaster ride of uncertainty. It was to my great relief and a lot of luck that so far there had not been a problem. And now Paul. He meant so much to me, yet despite his best efforts, I could not push the doubts and the worries away.

One evening in early November Paul dropped me off after a visit to the cinema. I stood on the drive and watched as the taillights of his car disappeared up the road and I suddenly felt very lonely and vulnerable, I was frightened. An awful fear of the unknown, of not knowing just what I had committed myself to. I panicked. Tears began to stream down my face as I ran back into the house. I sat down in my room unable to stop crying or shaking. A huge black hole was opening beneath me, and I could feel myself falling into it. What had I done? I felt so stupid for coming out, everything was so frightening.

Without really realising what I was doing I picked up the phone and dialled Paul's mobile. I could not get a coherent sentence out as he answered. He told me not to panic and to wait where I was, not to do anything silly, whatever that meant. Just four or five minutes later Paul came running in through the back door looking concerned. Without saying anything his arms pulled me to him, his hugs calmed me down and a minute later I was sitting shaking and feeling extremely foolish on a chair. A cup of coffee and a long, reassuring chat later and I got to bed much calmer and relieved at about three.

From then on, my outlook improved. Slowly I was accepting the fact that whilst I had lost Paul to Gary, I still had a strong and loyal friend. The jealousy – I would have to learn to cope with it. And so, we continued our regular trips to Wolverhampton on Saturday evenings. A slight conflict appeared one weekend in mid-November when my section officer phoned me one evening to ask if I would parade the following Sunday morning at eight, as they were expecting that there might be, of all things, a potential public disorder situation in, of all places, the church playing fields. I knew I was supposed to be going out to Gavan's with Paul and Gary the evening before but said yes to the duty.

Damn it, I would still go out! So, we went to Gavan's, and as I was not driving, I had drunk about four pints before leaving at two-thirty. By the time we had dropped Gary off and then Paul had driven over to Rugeley to drop me off, it was four-thirty and I got to bed at five. At seven-fifteen, I was woken by the alarm. I crawled out of bed, still mostly asleep, shivering because it was bloody cold and I was slightly hungover. I pulled on my uniform, zipped up my waterproof jacket and a few minutes later set out walking, in the freezing, sleety rain, towards the station. I vowed at once I would never, ever mix police duties and clubbing again. A few minutes later the door of the station banged shut behind me as I walked slowly and deliberately into the parade room. I sat down at the table and buried my head in my hands.

"Been clubbing again, have we?" asked one bright spark, I did not answer.

I spent the duty walking around in the rain with Steve Smith. As it turned out, there was not even a hint of any trouble, but at least I had Steve to talk to. It was still bothering me that Steve, one of the most honest people I knew, and one of my most trusted and loyal friends, still did not know that I was gay. I had to tell him as soon as possible.

One evening soon after, following a good evening in the Prince, we walked out to the car park. Steve had been asking about the club I was going to in Wolverhampton. We stood by the cars, talking. I had almost hinted at him but could not bring myself to say anything. I sensed that Steve was trying to say something too. As I got into the car to drive home, he hesitated and remained standing by the door, I wound down the window.

"What is it, Steve?"

"Oh, nothing, well nothing much," he replied.

I knew he wanted to say something, so I switched the engine off and got out of the car again.

"Go on Steve, what is it?"

"It's nothing, just something I'd heard, you know," his voice trailed off. We stood in silence for a few seconds until I could stand it no longer.

"Go on Steve, tell me, what have you heard?"

He laughed and shrugged his shoulders. He looked awkward, and I knew why.

"Is it about me?"

"Yeah…" His voice trailed again; he did not want to say it. I knew what he was trying to say.

"Is it about me being gay?"

He looked at me, relieved that I had broken the ice at last.

"Yes, that was it, not that it's any of my business of course. I'd just heard a rumour down the station."

"Well, it's true, I am gay. I'm just sorry I haven't told you before, I wanted to, but…"

This time it was my voice which trailed. Steve broke the ice this time.

"It doesn't matter to me mate, it's none of my business what you do. You're still a good mate to me."

I was relieved and slightly surprised that Steve had taken it so well. I was concerned that rumours were starting to circulate, but I was also, in a strange way, glad. Steve reassured me that he had not heard anybody saying anything derogatory about me. Even so, I could not help noticing an uneasy, queasy feeling deep inside that I had now started something over which I now had no control. I had pushed the door open and there was no way I could pull it shut if things did not work out. The same feeling as when you sit on a roller coaster, and it climbs slowly up the ramp before a big drop. Exhilaration and excitement mixed equally with real fear. Except that, on a rollercoaster, you know what is coming. I did not.

Chapter 7

Paying the Price

As Christmas 1992 approached I came to accept the fact that I would never have a relationship with Paul. Instead, a growing realisation and trust that I had at last and at least forged a close and strong friendship with someone in the same situation as me, boosted my confidence, and that finally, I was dragging myself out of the rut I had been stuck in for far too long. There seemed to be no problem at the station now that some of my friends and colleagues knew the truth, knew that I was gay. Yet again, it only went to boost my confidence, with one or two reservations I did not mind who knew now, I was enjoying the experience.

There was one concern that kept nagging at me. I did not know how any of the local troublemakers and criminals would react if they found out I was gay. How would it affect my effectiveness to do the job? I had no way of knowing but was determined that it was not going to be a problem for me. If they took issue with my sexuality, it would be *their* problem, and I would continue to do the job professionally as I had always done. Even so, I was concerned enough not to want my sexuality to be quite such public knowledge.

My only other concerns were my parents and my grandmother. Just the thought of saying anything to them instantly brought me out in a cold sweat, I could not handle that, I was not ready.

One evening Paul visited and we picked up my section officer Sarah. We drove over to Stafford for a quiet drink and a chat. It was an enjoyable evening which increased my confidence that my sexuality was not going to be a problem for me at the station. Here I was socialising with my gay friend and a colleague from the station who knew we were both gay. The two sides of my life were finally together.

As the build-up to Christmas increased, I began to think about the season. For one thing, my shift was not working Christmas day for the first time in two or three years, so I was quite relieved to have the day off!

My social life, having been boosted dramatically over the previous three months, was reflected in the number of hours I was now working at the station. Still much higher than the average amount of time specials put in, much higher than any other special at the station, but a lot less than I had been putting in. The station Christmas party at the Prince of Wales was only a few days away. I was still riding high on a wave of Euphoria and took the crazy decision to invite Paul along with me. Many of the other officers and staff took their partners along so why shouldn't I?

As in previous years, the lounge of the Prince of Wales was packed exclusively with police staff and friends by mid-evening. Paul and I walked into the middle of it, and I was proud that I had a close friend with me for once. Paul's face lit up as we walked in, and he could not resist commenting on the fact that there were *so many men!* It was overheard.

As we pushed our way through the crowd, I introduced Paul to those colleagues who 'knew' about me and had heard of Paul, and we chatted for a while with Sarah and Colin. It was as though, at last, I was being accepted in a society I had felt excluded from for so long. As the evening progressed and I had more to drink I relaxed more. Relaxed that at last, my sexuality was not a problem, I was here in the middle of a police social gathering at a pub in the middle of Rugeley, socialising with my gay friend – albeit not my partner, with a growing feeling of well-being and peace with the world.

The party became, as police socials can often get, quite rowdy and exuberant by the end of the evening. We slipped out of the back door of the pub around midnight in high spirits and set off, staggering slightly, back to my house, Paul was stopping the night.

Christmas was quiet. Paul called round for a few minutes on Christmas morning so that we could exchange presents, otherwise, I spent the day with my family.

New Year's Eve was going to be different; we had bought tickets a few weeks earlier for Gavan's and I was looking forward to it. As it turned out, the club was even more brash than usual with party poppers and balloons everywhere, some people came in fancy dress – (one or two men came in fancy dress as a matter of course anyway). Midnight came and ushered in what I confidently believed and hoped would be a year in which my life would change forever.

After Midnight we were back, fighting for a space to move in the middle of the dance floor. There was a tap on my shoulder, I turned, and Deb was beaming back at me!

"Hi Steve, I thought it was you!"

"Hi, Deb! It's nice to see you here…" I hesitated before continuing, "…I thought I might see you in here one day!"

Deb grinned back but did not reply.

"Anyway, happy new year!" I continued.

"Happy New Year to you too. I'm with a group of friends,

I've got to go back to them now, best wishes and see you soon!"

We hugged and Deb vanished back through the crowd towards her friends. I turned back to Paul and Gary who were looking at me puzzled, Paul had not met Deb. My confidence was boosted even more now that I knew I was not alone amongst the officers from Rugeley who visited Gavan's! When I spoke to Deb a few days later at the station she told me she had had a similar reaction when she went back to her friends. They were curious about the fact that she had walked up to and kissed *a man*! When she then told them that I was a colleague from Rugeley, they panicked and disappeared rapidly; they were also colleagues from the same force.

My growing confidence and euphoria were checked a couple of days later. I was back on duty working nights and was alarmed to hear a rumour going around the station that the male friend I had taken to the station Christmas party had been wearing make-up. I could not imagine why or who could be saying this, Paul certainly did not wear make-up, never to my knowledge had or ever would, he was not like that. Why spread a rumour like that?

It became obvious to me that it had originated from one of the officers whom I had not yet spoken to personally and was playing on the rumours going around the station about my sexuality. It fitted straight into their stereotypes of what gay men were like. The fact that quite plainly Paul or I were not like that did not matter, they just invented it. It was a worrying development; I had been going out of my way to spread the truth about myself and dispel any myths. I would have to re-double my efforts to speak to the rest of the officers I had not got around to telling yet.

A few days later Colin, one of the section officers, asked to speak to me in private. I was puzzled, as Colin already knew and had perfectly accepted me being gay, but it was not about him. Several officers had approached him since the Christmas party and were asking him whether the rumours they had heard about me were true. He had not wanted to break confidence so had not said anything to confirm it, he thought he ought to let me know.

That Christmas party was proving to be a pivotal event, a landmark in my 'coming out' journey. I just hoped that I would be able to speak to as many officers as possible before the rumours got out of hand. I told Colin that from now on he was free to tell anyone who asked him, it would make it easier for me.

So as the new year began, I embarked on my plan to tell as many people as possible. Unfortunately, events overtook my plans and completely put a stop to them.

One Saturday a week or two later in mid-January, I was on duty once more with my adopted shift. The afternoon was quiet, after tea I was quite pleased when Andy Adams asked me to go out on patrol with him. I had not found a chance to speak to Andy yet, this might be a good opportunity. As it turned out, we did not have much time to talk in the brief time we were out, and I was frustrated and a bit annoyed when we returned to the station an hour later. I did not get a chance then either because the sergeant had asked me to help in the control room for the rest of the evening.

I settled myself down to work in the control room. I quite enjoyed working in the control room because the work could be just as unpredictable as actually being out on patrol. Often it would be much busier, with responsibilities to control and check all the patrols via the radio base station, dealing with telephone enquiries, personal callers at the hatch, other officers calling in and messages sent via the computer system.

The evening started quietly; Colin arrived soon after to take a new, probationary constable out on patrol. After booking their radios out they set off into the town centre. The evening progressed quietly, giving me breathing space to think and chat with Ian. I was troubled with thoughts about how I would get around to dealing with all the rumours circulating about me and Paul on the other shifts. I was beginning to sense a slight resistance towards me from one or two quarters, not officers on my shift, but officers in the same station, nevertheless. Overall, though, my decision, to be honest, was working far smoother than I had dared hope. But I realised that I would have to act quickly now to dispel any unwarranted and false rumours.

Mid evening, after a quiet first half of the evening, Ian went off to the kitchen to brew a pot of tea for the shift. The phone rang, it was Pete, a DC from Cannock who had been a PC at Rugeley and it was good to speak to him again. Surely, he must have heard the rumours about me, I thought, as we chatted over the phone. But if he had, he said nothing and gave nothing away, we got on just as we had always done.

The control room radio crackled; I half-heard a garbled message from Colin in my other ear as I talked to Pete on the phone. I paused to listen, but the radio went quiet again. Anyway, it was not my responsibility now the station was effectively also being controlled from Cannock – the very room where Pete was speaking to me from now; they should have also heard the message. I noticed that no one responded to Colin's message, I was about to mention it to Pete when there was a further message as the radio crackled into life again.

"This is Whisky Bravo four two, TEN-NINE the taxi rank,Anson Street! Can we have some help please!" The voice was urgent.

My pulse was racing, Colin was shouting a 'ten-nine' call

from just up the road – that was an officer in distress who needed urgent assistance, but still, Cannock had not responded! I had to say something.

"Pete, has no one heard that ten-nine shout from Colin? I've got to go, speak to you soon!"

I put the phone down, and picked up the transmitter in our control room,

"Whisky Bravo to all patrols, there's a ten-nine call, the taxi rank, Anson Street!"

Dropping the transmitter, I ran to the door of the control room and shouted to anyone in the station within earshot, that there had been a ten-nine shout down the road. I grabbed a radio, pulled my tunic on, did not bother with my cap and ran out of the front door, desperately worried what trouble Colin and the new officer might be in to call in a ten-nine.

I soon found out. As I ran up Anson Street, I could see a group of agitated people standing around the grass bank near the taxi rank; as I got closer, I could see that someone was fighting in the middle of the group. Colin and the probationer were struggling with a youth, several of their drunk friends were standing around jeering and provoking more trouble.

Another officer was running towards them from the opposite direction, and as I got close Jeff drove past me and screeched to a halt in his patrol car.

For his size – a thin lanky teenager, the youth was putting up a formidable struggle; the probationer had a bleeding nose and Colin was on the ground rolling around with the youth, obviously having been assaulted himself. I pushed my way in, shoving drunken kids aside. Within a few seconds I was rolling around struggling with the youth too, he had phenomenal strength for his size and the struggle to subdue and restrain him was becoming epic. He seemed to be high on drugs – if he'd been drunk, he would have been extremely easy to restrain. My radio fell apart in the struggle. In between breaths and between blows aimed at both of us, Colin managed to tell me that the youth had been fighting with a girl when they had found them, and when he tried to intervene the youth had turned on Colin and as Colin had pulled him to the ground the youth managed to kick Colin in the head. Another car screeched to a halt and another couple of bobbies jumped out, in the struggle I couldn't even make out who had turned up, I could only see their boots, but patrols were arriving from all over the place now. Eventually, after a lot of effort and a titanic struggle with the youth, we managed to roll him over and I managed to get my handcuffs on both his wrists, which was a relief as I was running out of energy! He was arrested for assaulting a police officer.

Whilst other officers pushed the growing crowd to one side and dispersed them, I helped carry the still struggling youth towards the open rear door of the patrol car. Jeff ran around to the far door and opened it. It took a further minute of struggling to force the still-violent youth onto the back seat of the car. Several youths were standing around the police car goading our prisoner. Having fed him horizontally into the car and onto the back seat, Jeff held down his shoulders whilst I climbed into the back nearside and knelt on the youth's legs to stop him from flailing around and kicking. Another police officer tried to push the rear door shut, but the youth kicked out; I reached over and grabbed his leg, and with difficulty pulled it back into the car. The door was slammed shut and Jeff got back into the driving seat to leave me pinning the youth down, and in that instant, as Jeff turned the car around in a quick U-turn back towards the station, we both fell against the back of the front seats and the youth managed to pull his legs free of my hold.

Thud! My head was kicked and it hit the rear door pillar so hard that it left me dazed, then before I could get any senses back another hard kick. Then another, kick after kick. The youth was kicking me with all his strength and I was pinned against the pillar, utterly helpless. Yet I was completely silent; mute. I was being killed; the youth was going to cave my skull in I was certain. I put up my arms to try and deflect the kicks. Crunch! A vicious kick to my chest and I felt a sickening intense pain, then another even more sickening and painful kick, so as I tried to deflect the blows to my torso, the kicks were then aimed back to my head. It was becoming seriously dangerous.

I was completely unable to move or to free myself. Blow after blow collided with me, as hard as the youth could kick, against my face, my neck, and my chest; the youth was trying to kill me for certain now and I became frightened that he might succeed. I had to find some way of stopping him quickly! There was a searing, stabbing pain in the centre of my chest, it was extremely difficult to breathe and I was giddy from the blows to my head. I could not think with any clarity apart from the certain knowledge that if I did not stop him soon, I wasn't going to survive this. I *had* to stop the youth somehow. It was taking forever to reach the station, but it could be no more than about thirty seconds in reality. Suddenly there was an opportunity and I seized it. In that split second, as the youth had both legs away from me, I collapsed with all my weight on top of him, the adrenaline hardly masking the intense pain which shot across my chest as my full weight fell on him. I had gained the advantage, so as Jeff reversed the patrol car into the station yard, the youth was pinned. Done.

The car stopped; Jeff jumped out and opened the rear

passenger door on his side. I lay across the youth, panting, adrenaline surging, and the stabbing pain clouding my thoughts, I felt both dizzy and sick. Extremely poorly. Someone unseen pulled the door open behind me and I was hugely relieved. Fresh air! Another officer climbed in past Jeff from the other side and between them, the youth was dragged from underneath me, still kicking, and screaming obscenities. He even managed a final kick to my head, but I couldn't even stop him now. Still screaming, the youth was led off towards the already-opened door of the charge room where the custody sergeant would be waiting for him. The shouts and screams receded until finally, all I could hear was my own fitful, laboured breathing and then coughing. Spits of blood landed on my hand as I coughed and then realised with another shock a warm trickle of blood was dripping from my mouth. I was shaking uncontrollably.

I lay slumped against the back seat completely ignored and abandoned by the other officers. It was so quiet after the pandemonium of the past few minutes. I was breathing with great difficulty; the pain was the most intense and stabbing I had ever felt. Another cough, more blood. Panicking, I realised something was very wrong. I was dying. I had to get help, I had to get into the station, to tell someone. I didn't want to die here, on my own, in the back of a patrol car. Why had they all abandoned me?

I wriggled and pushed with all my will power and effort and tried to step out from the back seat, but my legs gave way and I fell out of the car in a heap onto the tarmacked car park. I lay there shaking, the grit on the ground stuck to my face but I didn't care, it wasn't important. Another excruciating cough: a small puddle of my blood was forming on the tarmac. I managed to pull myself upright with extreme difficulty, using the car door to help, but had to lean against the car to steady myself for a few seconds before setting off as my legs were extremely wobbly. I felt utterly confused, this was so far removed from real life it was frightening me. The intense sharp pains almost doubled me up. But I could see the still open, beckoning doorway into the charge room where there would be people who could help me. I staggered across the station yard. Anyone who might see me would think I was very drunk, but I didn't care. Several times I had to steady myself against the wall as my legs started to buckle but I had to get to someone who would help me, I couldn't collapse here.

I stepped into the charge room. It seemed strange, almost dreamlike, very vivid, overly bright, it didn't seem real, and I was getting double vision; I couldn't focus. It was like I was not there, as if I was just a spectator in a strange sort of horror film. Could no one see how I was? They seemed not to, but then I realised with a thrill of dismay that the charge room was empty. They must have taken the youth straight to the cells.

Help was now even further away, I now had to get to the cell corridor. I staggered and aimed for the left wall of the charge room. Mostly sliding along the wall to steady myself I managed to get out of the charge room. After what seemed like an age, I had passed the interview room and the stairs and eventually, I stepped into the cell corridor. Several officers were standing outside the first cell, including Colin and the probationer. The sergeant was in the cell with another officer trying to subdue the youth. Sarge looked up.

"Bloody Hell! Get out Steve, just get out now! We can manage!" he shouted.

I didn't argue, I could hardly speak; Sarge had seen the state I was in, I thought, Sarge knew I needed help! I backed back out into the custody corridor, leaning against the wall outside the cell, struggling with the pain and trying to stay upright. I was shaking and couldn't stop it yet I felt so stupid! I was letting the side down!

But I needed help, urgently; I knew I couldn't carry on much longer. Colin was standing opposite looking at me slightly shocked. I looked across at him, silently pleading for him to help me.

"Colin...help me!" I eventually gasped, between the stabbing pain. I staggered forward, putting my hand on his shoulder and felt my legs giving way and I again felt so ashamed.

"Bloody hell Steve, someone grab his other arm!" Colin replied, grabbing my arm tightly as my knees buckled and an inky grey was starting to spread across my vision, which I was fighting. I didn't want to die. I felt several unseen hands take hold of me and vaguely I was aware of being led up the corridor, then a few seconds later I was propped up in a chair back in the control room I had left only a few minutes earlier.

I felt sick. Voices unseen were asking me questions, but I could not work out who was speaking or even what they were asking, now; I just sat there shaking, hurting, and feeling I was about to vomit, unable to tell anyone how scared I was or how much I was hurting. I could vaguely hear someone behind saying something about calling an ambulance. Someone was kneeling in front of me looking at me with a concerned expression, speaking something, I couldn't hear them properly; but I had to tell someone what had happened. I tried pointing to and hitting the palm of my hand against my head and the left side of my chest,

"Kicked me – lots of times!" I managed to splutter with difficulty, and I thought – I hoped – that they understood. I felt stupid but I could barely see now, I was extremely nauseous, and I began to salivate, saliva dripping onto the floor mixed with blood. It was frightening me. Suddenly I was falling forward out of the chair, still falling, a very strange sensation like I was flying and I became aware of several hands supporting me again and I thought I was being carried out of the control room, and then everything went very hazy but for one clear thought: Sarge needs my keys! Then nothing more.

The next clear impression I had, that I became slowly conscious of, was movement. Bumpy movement. I lay still for a moment trying to work out where I was, and what was happening. I opened my eyes. I was lying in the back of an ambulance. I raised my head up a bit. An oxygen mask pressed against my face, my blood-stained shirt unbuttoned and open, and pads attached to my chest, and I could feel something squeezing the end of a finger. I tried to pull myself up further, but a hand very gently pushed me back down. A calming, reassuring, unseen voice was telling me I was going to be OK, that they were looking after me and squeezed my hand, and most importantly, I believed them. I was safe and maybe I wasn't going to die. I had forgotten about the keys. No more thoughts.

Several hours later, sometime the following morning, I eventually woke up. Complete disorientation and panic for about thirty seconds, wondering why I was lying in a hospital bed, until jumbled memories from the night before started to form, disjointed and out of order, but at least these calmed me down, at least I felt alive again! I could breathe easier although I could feel my chest was extremely sore. More than anything else I could properly see again, I didn't feel sick, and I wasn't spitting blood. A nurse was fussing around and noticed I'd woken up.

"Ah, you're back with us Steven!" she said, smiling and fussing around me.

"How long have I been here?" I croaked.

"I think you were brought in about ten o'clock last night, but

I wasn't on duty then. I think we were quite worried about you when you arrived but it wasn't as serious as it could easily have been! I heard that you were kicked several times trying to make an arrest?"

"Something like that, I think…" I replied, smiling back at her. I could only remember fragmented episodes from the incident the night before.

"I thought I was going to die…" I said almost apologetically, my voice trailed off.

"But you didn't, did you?" She squeezed my hand, looking at me with a very concerned expression.

"You're going to be fine; I promise." She smiled at me.

"I'll go and let the doctor know you're awake and he wants to come and see you", with another smile, she turned to go but I called her back.

"Er, what time is it now?"

"Just after ten a.m.," she said, smiling before she turned again and left the cubicle.

I lay back staring at the ceiling and wondered what had happened to the last twelve or more hours. I did remember how frightened I'd been – but I was now much calmer, I really didn't feel like I was dying. I was still feeling quite groggy so I closed my eyes and fell into a peaceful sleep.

A doctor eventually came to see me, and he explained that they had been really worried about me the night before. They thought I'd got a bleed on my brain and blue-lighted me to hospital, but a scan showed it was a slight swelling of my brain due to it being shaken about in my skull from the kicking; I had a very severe concussion but no bleeding, so they had kept me sedated for several hours. The bleeding had been from a cut in my mouth and was now stitched – I had already become aware of the soreness and stitches.

Five ribs were cracked on my left side, and I had something called costochondral separation where the ribs were pulled away from the cartilage which attaches them to the sternum. That was the searing pain I had felt in the middle of my chest. The doctor explained that the police station had rung a couple of times to check up on me. That pleased me.

More than anything else, I was so relieved I had come through it all with no serious injuries and extremely grateful to all those who'd looked after me. Pending a check-up later in the morning I should be able to go home later that day! I was told that I would have to stay off full police duties for six weeks but maybe just some light duties after a week or so, until my ribs fully healed. When I was left alone again, I fell again into a deep but relaxing sleep.

I was eventually discharged and allowed home later. A nurse helped me to get dressed back into my uniform, which I was struggling with due to the pain from my cracked ribs, but shortly after I was sitting in the waiting room of Stafford District General Hospital waiting for my lift home. My uniform was in tatters; buttons were hanging by a thread, and one of my tunic pockets was hanging loose, something which bothered me as I took so much pride in being smart in my uniform. I was in a state of shock but *very* relieved to still be alive! I was badly bruised I discovered; I was hurting all over from the assault and I was told the concussion might not totally clear for several days at least. A nurse called Rugeley Police Station for me, to sort out a lift back to Rugeley.

Fortunately, the waiting room wasn't too busy, but I was getting a few strange looks. I leaned forward and put my head in my hands to avoid looking at anyone. I was desperately trying to remember exactly what had happened the previous evening but there were huge gaps in my memory of the incident. The doctor had warned me this might happen but still it was unsettling. I had a dull headache developing too. A receptionist was standing beside me suddenly. I looked up...

"Hello Mr Johnson, I have just had a call that a police officer from Stafford will pick you up shortly."

I thanked her and went back to staring at the floor below me, trying to avoid the quizzical looks from others in the waiting room. I must have looked like a pathetic mess!

A few minutes later a traffic officer walked into the waiting room, dispatched from traffic headquarters to deliver me back to Rugeley, and I was extremely glad to see him. He helped get me upright and very gingerly I followed him out into the fresh air. I asked him to drop me off at the police station.

My one consolation, I thought on the way back to Rugeley, was that the youth was still securely locked in my handcuffs. No one else at the station had a key to match and they'd have had to wait for my return or collect them!

The driver delivered me to the car park at the back of the station twenty minutes later, declined a cuppa and set off back to Stafford after I'd thanked him profusely. I let myself in via the back door and made my way to the parade room. Joe looked up from his paperwork:

"Steve, you're back! How are you?" he jumped up and was grinning. "It's good to see you back again! – Sarge! Come through, Steve's back!"

Sarge stuck his head around the door of his office, beaming. He came in and sat opposite on the other side of the parade room table. I sat down too, carefully.

"Go and put the kettle on Joe, I'm sure Steve would

appreciate a drink."

Joe got up and headed for the kitchen. I sat fiddling with the hospital tag still on my wrist.

"So, tell me how you are Steve. We were all really worried about you last night, you really did frighten us, you looked extremely unwell!"

"Sarge, I can promise you that I felt it! I'm OK I think, but aching all over." Then in a low voice, almost ashamed to say it, "I thought I was dying, Sarge!" I looked down at the table, ashamed to look up. "I don't have much memory of what happened after the assault though."

"I didn't think you would have Steve, you looked like you were on another planet when I saw you in the cell! Soon after that, you were pretty much away with the fairies, as they say. To say we were a bit worried would be an understatement!" He looked across at me with a concerned expression. I sat, self-consciously fiddling with the tag.

"When the ambulance arrived, they were worried that you really might have a life-threatening brain injury, the way you slowly lost consciousness…"

We sat looking at each other silently for a while, lost in our own thoughts. Joe came back with a tray full of very welcome cups of tea for us and the controller. I looked back at Sarge.

"I've got five cracked ribs on my left side and something called costochondral separation."

"What on earth is that?" asked Joe, sitting down next to me.

"Ribs pulled away from the cartilage on my breastbone, I think," I replied.

"Ouch! That sounds painful!" replied Joe.

"It really is, Joe! Excruciating at times, when I least expect it." I looked across at Sarge.

127

"Sarge…I have got to have six weeks off active duties! I'm sorry about that!"

"You don't have to apologise, Steve."

"I think I can do light duties here though," I continued, hopefully. I looked up at Sarge. He was smiling at me.

"Don't worry Steve, at least you're okay now, and we're all very relieved it wasn't as serious as we thought it was. Also, don't worry about your lost memory of it, I'm sure it will come back soon, although it might be better if it didn't, don't you think?"

"That's what the doctor told me too, Sarge." and I smiled.

Suddenly, I remembered about my handcuffs…

"Sarge, is that youth still in my handcuffs?"

Sarge just continued looking at me, smiling.

"What do you think Steve?" he said eventually.

"He must be, Sarge! No one had a key for them apart from me!"

He was grinning now.

"Where's your key then?"

I felt, very carefully, in the top right pocket of my tunic. It was empty. I must have lost it sometime in the arrest and assault or afterwards. Sarge saw that I was looking slightly panicked.

"Sarge!"

Now he was laughing. He reached under the table, revealed and pushed my handcuffs – and my key – across the table to me. I looked at him blankly.

"Did you think we would let you go off in the ambulance without retrieving your key? We found it before they took you away in the ambulance! We searched your pockets until we found it…"

I smiled. Of course! I felt stupid. A very welcome cup of tea calmed me down again, and even though I was warned not to have any hot drinks for a few hours, I needed it. Joe drove me home shortly after.

I could not lie down easily; the pain in my ribs was intense if I lay on my left side and it would take weeks to heal. I devised a system of putting pillows behind me when lying on my right side, to stop me from rolling over through the night. There was no way I could go back on full duty for a while now, not until my ribs had healed. I popped into the station a day later for photographs to be taken of the injuries and to write up a statement of everything I could remember. I did manage a couple of light duties working in the control room a week later when I had recovered sufficiently, but even that, I soon found, was quite difficult; I would have to take it easy. For the time being at least, it had put an end to my plan to stop the rumours.

In the meantime, as I started my recovery, I focused on my personal life again. I answered another advertisement in the paper and met Andy. He lived locally. We got on well and became good friends, although still completely mixed up about Paul, I couldn't see us forming a relationship; our friendship was not like that. I had at least made another good friend. And Andy had another gay friend who lived a few miles away in Lichfield.

One evening Andy took us over to Lichfield to meet Mike. He was a pleasant and interesting person; in his spare time, he worked as a counsellor for a gay helpline, and he was interested in my experiences with the police. He knew a gay police officer who worked for the same counselling organisation in London, Ian was also a member of the Lesbian and Gay Police Association. I had seen it advertised before and was interested, so Mike said he would give Ian my phone number the next time he spoke to him. By the time we left later that evening, I was feeling much more positive. I was building up a rapidly growing circle of gay friends.

Yet things were not OK. I noticed I was becoming increasingly stressed and I was slightly depressed. I wasn't sleeping well, and not just because my ribs were still extremely painful. I couldn't concentrate, I was becoming paranoid too. Something was still not right with Paul, certainly. I couldn't put my finger on it, but I knew something was wrong. We still got on well, but since Christmas, there was a slight distance between us, I couldn't work out what the problem was, and it began to unsettle me again. Even so, I couldn't understand why I was getting so much anxiety now. I couldn't think of any reason why I was feeling like this. What was going on?

As the weeks slowly passed, my ribs healed allowing me to sleep again properly, and I once more started to think about returning to work but I found myself teetering ever closer to the edge of that black pit again. Being depressed as I was now becoming, was awful. My life was so uncertain, I became worried about officers at the station, my career was still not sorted, and I was worried about Paul.

We continued going out to Gavan's though, one evening we even ventured up to Manchester for a change. On one trip to Gavan's, we were slightly early getting to Wolverhampton, so we called into a gay pub just around the corner from the club. The bar was crowded but we managed to squeeze into it. I was scanning the people standing in front of me towards the bar when my sight stopped on a neck two or three bodies ahead of me. I recognised it. I could not be certain; he had his arms around another bloke standing next to him. No, it couldn't be! But then he turned and saw me. It was John, my friend in the specials from Wombourne! He looked over, saw me, and looked surprised.

"What are *you* doing *here*!" he asked.

I thought for several seconds, grinning at him.

"I think for the same reason that you're here!" I replied.

In all the years I had known John since we trained together as probationers, I had never guessed or even imagined he might be gay himself. He often had a girlfriend with him at socials and parties. But then again, so had I and probably – no, obviously now, for the same reason. We went over to the club together as a group and I spent some time talking to John in a quiet corner. It helped to calm my fears about the rumours at the station. Two officers I had known for some time I now knew were gay, although I had to admit, neither of them had taken the plunge and 'come out' to their colleagues as I had done. I asked John what his station was like to work at. He enjoyed working there, and the inspector in charge was very much in favour of the specials. John was not actually 'out' at his station, but he did not seem too concerned whether he was.

By the end of February, I was ready to resume duties. I returned to the station worried about what my position would be like there but was relieved to find that everything seemed to be as I had left it – at least as far as the officers I worked with, I did not know about any others. I was told we were about to have a new inspector in charge at Rugeley, at last. Ever since Inspector Cooper had left, two or three years earlier, we had seen a succession of temporary officers in charge of the station. It was affecting morale. I was pleased to learn that the new inspector was to be Inspector Robertson, currently in charge of John's station down at Wombourne. I was pleased that we were to have an inspector who was so very in favour of the special constabulary.

I started to think about cutting down the number of hours I

was working. From now on I would concentrate on finding another career, but once again I did not know where. In the meantime, I returned to active duties at the station and was soon back on the job, properly.

Inspector Robertson moved up to the station at the beginning of April, I was keen to meet him, having heard such good reports about him from John. I got the chance when he took the parade one afternoon at the start of the shift a week later. After signing our pocket notebooks at the end of the parade he caught me in the corridor outside the parade room.

"Ah! Steve. I am glad to catch you. I have heard about all the work you have done down here since you joined, you have certainly put in an impressive amount of time, and you give us a lot of support. I am busy now, but I hope we have time for a chat soon to get to know each other, I am very much in favour of the special constabulary, you do a fantastic job. Pop in for a chat soon when you're free."

"Thank you, I will do, sir."

We shook hands and he strode off towards his office. I walked down towards the control room to book my radio out, smiling to myself full of optimism, pleased that at last, we had another decent officer in charge.

Everything was getting back on course again, my social life had certainly improved out of all recognition, but that only served to highlight my lack of progress elsewhere. Still, I could not work out why Paul was being so evasive to my questioning when I asked him what was wrong. That something was not right between us I was now certain, although I couldn't say exactly what it was. All sorts of reasons sprang to mind. I was putting too much pressure on Paul, perhaps he did not want to remain friends but could not bring himself to say so. Was it because I had not got another job away from policing?

As the weeks passed and winter gave way to spring, I became increasingly unhappy, with anxiety levels extremely high, depressed, and uncertain about just everything in my life, and with difficulty sleeping well too, even though my ribs were healing, I decided to confront Paul. On a fateful Wednesday evening in mid-April, I called Paul to try once again to ease my fears. Of course, it was all about Paul, but it was all I could focus on. My parents had gone away for a few days, and it made it easy to talk over the phone. It did not go well though. I knew something was wrong, but Paul just fell silent when questioned, it only made things worse. I was increasingly certain that there was now a problem with our friendship. Was Gary putting pressure on him not to see me, or was I being paranoid? Paul had been, by his own admission, the catalyst which had dragged me out of the closet all those months ago. I had never met anyone before who had been so much of an influence on me, affected my life so much, and given me so much hope. Now I was worried about the consequences of my actions in 'coming out' at the station. My life had drastically changed there. Suddenly I felt very vulnerable, I was on the edge of that bottomless black hole again, and I was panicking. Had I opened the closet door too far and too soon?

I tried again to find out what was wrong with Paul, but we were getting nowhere. The pressure was unbearable, and I could think of nothing else to say or worth asking. I was gasping for breath, and panicking; I needed to get off the phone as I could tell I was about to have a panic attack.

"I'm sorry Paul, I've had enough of this, I can't cope with this conversation just now." I put the receiver down on him; I was not in the right frame of mind to carry on talking to Paul.

I slumped into a chair and curled up, shaking, very frightened about the predicament I was in. I was suddenly very unsure about the decision I had taken to 'come out' to my colleagues, it might have been better if I had not met Paul at all and instead gone on performing regular duties and drinking in the Prince with Steve. I tried to calm my fears down again. I thought for a few seconds and realised that was all in the past now. No, I had not made a mistake, I could not go back to that again and it was too late now anyway. I calmed down. My life certainly had improved drastically. More than anything else, I reminded myself that I was now much more certain and happier about *who* I was. I would never be ashamed of that again. I sat in the chair, numb and drained emotionally.

The back door was abruptly flung open and a few seconds later Paul came bounding into the room, quite pale and breathless; he seemed very worried. Without saying anything he knelt in front of me and put his arms around me, pulling me forward, and hugging me close to him.

"I was so worried about you Steven; I thought you were going to do something stupid when you put the phone down on me…"

It had never occurred to me that he might have taken my last statement like that, and it shocked me, but not half as much as his next statement.

"I think you ought to know Steve, that I phoned the police; they'll be here in a minute. I'm surprised they did not get here before I did. I was really worried about you and I thought they would get to you sooner than I could, and you certainly sounded like you needed help" he said, almost apologetically. "I *do* care very much about you Steven; you will not lose my friendship."

Paul pulled me to him again as I apologised about what I had said, I reassured him that I had not intended or even thought of it that way. Now the police were coming, that was the last thing I wanted. A car pulled up outside.

"That'll be them now, I'll just go and have a word."

I heard voices in the kitchen as I composed myself; I felt stupid. A couple of minutes later a sergeant from one of the other shifts and Jenny, a WPC who I had worked with before, walked in looking overly concerned.

I explained to them that I was fine and that I was not going to do anything stupid; I was keen to explain how Paul had taken what I'd said the wrong way. I told them I was worried about my current situation and lack of a job, and the stress caused by the events of the past few months had taken its toll. To my surprise, Jenny did not know anything about my relationship with Paul, the fact that he was gay and more to the point, that I was too. So, it had not filtered through to everyone yet. But Jenny seemed perfectly fine about it all.

Before leaving the sergeant came and had a private word. He suggested I ought to have a few days off, not to feel obliged to come on duty and he suggested I should have a chat with the force welfare officer. He was sorry that it had happened like this, but there was no way that he could hide what had happened this evening from the rest of the station, it was an incident logged on the computer. I knew the implication of what he was saying, I would be gossiped about by everyone at the station now, it certainly was not going to make my job of 'coming out' any easier, but it was too late to change that now.

They left a few minutes later satisfied that I was OK. I agreed to go to the station the following morning to see the sergeant. Paul came back in after they had left, and we sat and talked over a cup of coffee which he had made. The shock of what had just happened was just sinking in. At least Paul reassured me that our friendship was intact, he apologised for the way he had been evasive, but I still got no nearer to finding out what had been the problem. We sat silently, awkwardly, for a few seconds, staring at each other. Finally, it was Paul who broke the ice:

"You need a break, Steven," he said quietly.

"Yes, I know, I *really do* need a break now."

I thought about what had just happened and came out in a cold sweat. My life had taken a violent lurch sideways. I did need a break now. I thought about it for a few seconds.

"Mum and Dad have bought a caravan in North Wales. Would you fancy a weekend there soon?" I asked, hopefully.

"Yes absolutely, that sounds perfect!"

The relief was obvious on my face; Paul had noticed and smiled. He gave me another hug.

By the time Paul left an hour later, I felt much calmer, and the future was not as bleak as I had thought. Yet as I drifted asleep that night, I was troubled by the reaction I would get when I visited the station later.

I walked down to the station after breakfast. I found the sergeant I had seen the previous evening and he seemed pleased that I was much happier than he had seen me the night before. Again, he suggested that I should consider having some time off duty, not to worry about any commitments, but to spend the time looking for a job and he reiterated his suggestion that it might be good to have a chat with the force welfare officer. I said I would think about it, but I did not know how he might be able to help me. I had only met Rob Williams once before when he had spoken to me and Dave soon after a fatal road accident which we had attended several years earlier. The sergeant told me he would have to speak to my section officer and SDO, and they would contact me in the next few days.

I left the station relieved that the whole incident was blowing over, it would not be as bad as I had feared. And my anxiety was eased a lot after the conversation with Paul. Anyway, a brief time off duty might be useful, it might give me the breathing space I need to start sorting my life out. The only problem I could see was the difficulty I now had in completing the task I had set out to do all those months before when I had begun talking to colleagues. Once again, I would be away from the station for a while, I could only hope now that any rumours would not get out of hand while I was away.

Two days later the SDO, Rob, phoned me at home. It was Rob whom I had fallen out with all those years earlier soon after joining and was now my SDO, in overall charge of the specials in Rugeley. He had to see me at some point, officially. We agreed he would call round to see me with the divisional commandant on the following Monday evening. I realised my parents would be back then, so I was quick to point out that they did not know that I was gay, and to be discreet when they came.

Right at the appointed time on the following Monday evening, the doorbell rang. I had warned my parents earlier that they were coming around, but I was careful not to say why.

Both Rob and Tony Haywood, the divisional commandant, were all smiles and politeness as I led them through the lounge, past my parents, and into my room at the back, where I was careful to close the door behind us. Rob was carrying files and a clipboard. After inviting them to sit, I settled myself, looking forward to the discussion, eager to show them how positive I was; that there were no problems.

"Well Steve, I hear you've had a few domestic problems, that's what we're here about," said Rob to get things going. Tony

137

smiled but said nothing.

"Yes, I know, I'm sorry about all that, but it really was all a big misunderstanding; my friend Paul took what I had said the wrong way, and I was *not* suicidal. My real concern is the fact that I haven't got a job, but also, I've been depressed and stressed for weeks and haven't got a clue why..." I was trying to be as bouncy and positive as I could manage without sounding false.

"Yes, we do understand that" said Tony, "and that's why we're here."

"Steven, we think it would be best for you to have some time off from duties. It will give you time to sort yourself out." continued Rob.

"OK..." I replied, hesitantly, this all seemed a bit too official suddenly, and I became worried, something about the tone of his voice. I believed they had come on a pastoral visit. I thought for a few seconds before continuing. This might be a good opportunity to kill two birds with one stone.

"I've also been a bit worried about the possible reaction from some of the officers at the station when I started to tell people...you know," I checked my parents could not hear before continuing, "...that I'm gay." in a low voice.

Rob and Tony looked at each other before continuing. Rob fumbled awkwardly with the papers he was holding.

"Yes, we want to talk to you about that also." I suddenly became alarmed, not so much at what Rob had said, but the way he had said it. Something definitely wasn't right. Tony continued:

"Steve, how would you react if other officers, quite naturally, found it difficult to accept that you are gay?"

I thought for a few seconds about what he had just said, what he was implying, and I became even more worried and then suddenly defensive.

"What do you mean?" I asked quietly but with a determined voice, "Are there any problems? I haven't been aware of any major problems with officers at the station."

"No, we're not saying there have been," said Rob, cutting me short. Tony joined in:

"Steve, as you know, we all work as a team. If we did not trust each other, it would be impossible to work effectively, and dangerous too…"

"On top of that, what about if you were injured on duty," Rob interrupted, "Some of the other officers might be worried about treating you, they might see you as a possible health risk."

I stared at him, finding it difficult to believe what I was hearing as he fumbled nervously with the papers he was holding. Now I was beginning to see the *real* reason for their visit! The recent assault had started this!

"One of the reasons we've been asked to speak to you, Steve, is to ask you whether you would be prepared to resign from the specials." Said Rob, suddenly much more formally.

I sat, staring, unbelieving, I could hardly think what to say, my mind was racing. Now the purpose of their visit was blatantly clear, I understood what the paper which Rob was nervously fumbling, was. They wanted me to sign a form resigning from the police – *because I was gay.* I stared at them both, unable to believe what I'd just heard. In that very instant, with my anger rising at an alarming rate, which I feared I would not be able to control for very much longer, my whole life changed, forever.

Suddenly, my easy journey of self-discovery, my 'coming out' had been turned on its head. Destroyed in one sentence. I was determined, from that moment on, that no one was going to force me out of Staffordshire Police then or at any time in the future *just because I was gay.*

I turned to Rob; I was remarkably calm.

"No." was the only reply I made, quietly but very decisively.

Rob looked at Tony for inspiration. Tony took over.

"Steve, we understand how you feel, but at a small station like Rugeley, everybody must be able to trust everybody else all the time. You've now got a potential problem by telling everyone that you are gay."

He paused waiting for a reply from me, I remained silent, staring, and still not able to take in what was happening. Realising I was not going to say anything, Tony continued, "At the very least, would you consider transferring to another station in the division."

My anger was welling up, and I was finding it difficult to keep calm now. I had to be very firm and decisive in my answer. Suddenly, so sudden it felt like being hit by an express train, my life had just been knocked right away from the course it had been heading until that evening. I became a new person. Gone was Steven as I knew him, the almost timid easy-going, gentle person I had been. Here was a new me, with a different agenda and outlook. How should this new me answer? I stared, unbelieving at what I'd just heard, from Rob to Tony and back to Rob again. Finally, I knew exactly what to say:

"Absolutely not!" I replied, very firmly but quietly, "And do not believe for *one second* that this is *my* problem. It is *your* problem to sort out if there is any conflict or problem at the station! No, I will *not* resign or accept a transfer." I paused before delivering the clinching statement. "The force had better not make my sexuality an issue, it has got nothing to do with the reason why you were supposed to visit me tonight."

There were several seconds of nervous silence whilst I

struggled to control my breathing. All the time I was very conscious of my parents who were sitting a few feet away in the lounge, watching the television and completely oblivious to what was going on and the huge turmoil going on for me. Rob broke the silence, his voice mollified by my last statement.

"Anyway, Steve, we've also come to inform you that you must take the next five weeks off duty on sick leave. You are *not* to go down to the station during that time, at the end of it we will review the situation. In the meantime, you have got to make an appointment to see the force welfare officer, Rob Williams. You will not be allowed back on duty until you have. Is that clear?"

"Yes, perfectly clear," I replied, shocked and subdued.

They both looked at each other and made to get up. As Rob turned to leave my room, he saw my parents in the lounge.

"By the way Steve, have you said anything to your parents yet?"

"No, I haven't, they still don't know."

"Well, I…we think it would be a good opportunity over the next five weeks to tell them."

My anger boiled over. I could not control it now. With barely disguised contempt I snapped back, yet quiet enough for my parents not to overhear:

"I'll tell my parents when it suits me, that is none of your bloody business! Get out now!" I pointed towards the door. And I never spoke another word to them that evening.

"Anyway Steve, we'll be off now," said Tony, awkwardly and obviously taken aback by my stance.

I followed them both back through the lounge. I did not know what to say or do as they stopped briefly to swap pleasantries with my parents as they passed through. How would my parents react if they knew what had just happened? I said nothing, indeed could say nothing but was seething inwardly. I led them through into the hall and opened the front door eager for them to get out. Rob turned to me one last time as they stepped outside.

"I'll be in touch over the next few weeks to see how you are."

I said nothing, merely staring contemptuously at him. They turned and walked away; I closed the door quietly.

As I walked back through the lounge my mother stopped me.

"What did they want?"

"Oh, nothing much, I just had to see them about... something," I said, pathetically.

She seemed satisfied, to my relief, with that. Quietly but deliberately, I walked through into my room, shut the door, and sat down on the floor in front of the fire. Inside I was seething, the anger and turmoil of such an intensity I had never felt before.

Now it was clear to me what was happening. The force had been waiting for an opportunity to get rid of me since they had found out I was gay; the incident a few days before had given them the perfect excuse, or so they thought. From how far up the chain of command had it come? All the doubts and uncertainties of the last few weeks were wiped away; inside now was a burning and solid conviction that they would *never* get rid of me because of my sexuality. Never. From that moment on my whole life changed course, yet I didn't realise it then.

It was late, and my parents were getting ready to go to bed. I continued sitting quietly on the floor, appearing to my parents, happy and contented. I even smiled at my mother and thanked her as she brought me a cup of tea before going up to bed.

The lounge was silent, dark, and empty. I did not move. Inside, my mind was working overtime, wondering what would happen now. It was as if battle lines had just been drawn up, and

I was now waiting for the battle.

Then I remembered how just a few months earlier the police had been my whole life, about the respect I had and the devoted service I had given for so long. And now this. Just because I was honest; because I had told my friends there that I was gay. I could not help being gay, I had not done it on purpose. They would not win. They *must* not win.

Then my eyes were burning. I lifted my hand to cover my face, almost ashamed of myself, but the tears kept coming. And then I sat and thought. I thought about lots of issues that were now affecting my life and had pushed it in a different direction. My parents were asleep in bed upstairs blissfully unaware of the torment I was going through. The tea was undrunk, cold.

Chapter 8

Feeling the Pressure

Determination. More than any other emotion, it was a determination not to let them get away with this which was left by the time I woke the next morning. The shock had subsided; I realised that I was not very shocked at all about the discrimination, for it was plainly discrimination. The most surprising aspect of the whole incident was how blatant they had been about their homophobia; they hadn't even been tactful.

Now I was effectively suspended, despite it officially being called *sick leave*. I couldn't go on duty, and I was told I could not even visit the station. This might, before this had happened, have puzzled me because it did not make sense without an ulterior motive. But I now realised that the real reason I had been suspended had nothing to do with my well-being. So why did they want to keep me away from the station? No other officer is barred from the station if they're on sick leave. I had an uneasy feeling it was something more sinister and guessed what it was. I had very effectively been cut off from my friends and colleagues for another five weeks at least – Rob had only told me they would review the situation then. What lies might have spread around the station by the time I returned?

And then there were my parents. I knew now that I had to speak to them at some point. It angered me that pressure was being put on me by the police; it was none of their business, and

I would do it in my own time. Yet, how was I going to explain to my parents why I was not going on duty? Surely, they were going to notice very soon.

My main concern now was to convince the police that nothing was wrong with me and to give them no excuse for continuing my suspension because I was on sick leave. Paul and I became closer again as if we were pulling together to fight the enemy. All the friends I had recently made were supporting me, which was good because I had been effectively cut off from my friends at the station. Having lost most of my friends from the caving group because of my role as a police officer, these friends were the only real friends I now had.

There was no way that I could keep out of touch with my friends at the station. If I could not visit, I would phone them. I phoned the station one afternoon when I knew my adopted shift was on duty and guessed Ian Gilbey would be in the control room. At least Ian would tell me anything which was being said there. I trusted him. But when I called him, I could sense that there was unease, which surprised me, but realised it was because other officers were standing nearby. He told me to call him later, I could tell there was something he wanted to tell me.

What Ian later told me was not very encouraging. He had heard that officers at the station were finding it difficult to accept me being gay; things were being said. Most importantly and shockingly, he went on to tell me that Inspector Robertson had paraded shift two a day or so earlier and had referred to gay people. What he had said to the shift left everybody there quite certain of his views about gay people. And, by extension, his views about me. *I was a disgusting pervert.* Ian seemed to think, in his dry, very understated way, that I was going to have a few problems with getting things sorted out now.

145

As I replaced the telephone handset, I thought the same and I was struck by the irony of what had just happened. John, my friend from Wombourne, had told me what a good inspector Robertson was, but of course, Robertson did not know that John was gay and John did not know about Robertson's homophobia and bigotry. The inspector had taken me aside to thank me for my support only a week or so earlier, he did not know I was gay at that time, and thus a disgusting pervert.

Because the officer in charge of the station thought the way he did, and so openly expressed his views to my colleagues on shift two whom he knew I worked with, I wondered whether I would ever get what was turning into a rapidly escalating problem sorted out satisfactorily. I became increasingly worried and desperate to prove that there was nothing wrong with me, that there was no reason they could stop me from going on duty any longer.

I was at least pleased that my social life was progressing well, it diverted my attention from my problems at the station. The strain of what was happening there was beginning to show. I had to keep myself occupied. I thought again about my parents, but I could not bring myself to say anything, I had no idea how to approach it.

As the weeks passed it became ever more obvious that I was being kept away from the station for reasons other than concern about my health. Despite saying he would keep regular contact to check how I was, Rob Rawles did not contact me at all. Apart from my calls to Ian Gilbey, I was completely cut off, and with an officer in charge of the station as openly homophobic as Robertson was, I was increasingly worried I was going to find it much harder to get back the longer this all went on.

One evening in mid-May, a month after my suspension, I

was surprised to get a phone call from Rob Rawles. He was checking to see how I was, and I was very quick to point out to him that there was absolutely nothing wrong with me and that I wanted to return to active duty as soon as possible. I had already had enough time off on sick leave this year! Rob asked again if I had told my parents, and once again I told him it was up to me when I said anything. I got the impression they were somehow going to use that against me going back on duty. Before ending the call, Rob reminded me to contact the force welfare officer, he ended by saying my situation would be reviewed at the end of May, in a couple of weeks.

I did not believe him; as I put the phone down, I realised I was becoming paranoid about what was happening, I no longer trusted what they were saying to me. Was I paranoid, or was I instead being realistically cautious?

The divisional commandant, Tony Haywood phoned later the same evening, surprised when I told him Rob had called me earlier, but it seemed too much of a coincidence that they had both called independently on the same evening. I told Tony exactly what I had told Rob, I had to get the message across that they could not realistically continue to keep me away on 'sick leave' for much longer. I knew they were going to try.

I was desperately in need of a holiday and all my remaining friends agreed. I mentioned the weekend at my parent's caravan which Paul had agreed to, and we arranged to go the following weekend. At least I could look forward to what would be a pleasant and much-needed break. Paul picked me up the following Saturday morning and we set off for Wales. I relaxed noticeably as we left Rugeley and then Staffordshire behind and headed towards the mountains.

We settled down in the caravan that evening after a day of

driving and walking around Snowdonia. I have always enjoyed the isolation and peace of mountains and it was a much-needed tonic now. But as it turned out, the weekend only made my anxiety worse. What was wrong with me? My position at the station was in doubt, I had lost most of my friends and now I was arguing with Paul again. I had never before argued with Paul like this though, it was obvious something was very wrong. Paul suddenly shouted that he'd had enough, he was going home. We reached a hiatus.

Without warning, Paul burst into tears, something I had never seen him do. I was frightened; something was seriously wrong; he was such a pitiful sight. My anxiety suddenly evaporated, I was immediately concerned for Paul, my emotions had switched off, and I was once again cold and professional. I knelt on the floor in front of him and held out my arms.

"Come here, come here," I said very quietly, gesturing.

Paul came and knelt in front of me, tears streaming down his face. I put my arms around him and pulled him to me, he was shaking violently.

"What is it, Paul? Please tell me, let me help!"

He pulled himself away slightly.

"Steve, I'm sorry, but it is really worrying me that you still want to stay in the police service. You were almost killed a few weeks ago and that frightened me! It *really* frightened me! I can't cope with it! I didn't know how I could tell you as I know how much it means to you."

I hadn't expected that.

"I'm so sorry," was all I said, pathetically and very quietly, trying to find an answer for him, trying I realised, to find an answer to that myself.

I pulled him closer and held him tightly again.

"Paul, I really don't know what the answer is. All I know now is that somehow, I have *got* to win this fight. I cannot let them get away with it. I must win. Maybe then I can rethink my position."

Paul hugged me tighter. I felt torn in two. Eventually, Paul let go and sat back. We sat in silence looking at each other for what seemed a long time, holding hands. It was Paul who spoke first.

"You haven't been well for weeks now" – he was very hesitant – "I don't know what it is, but something isn't right with you Steve."

I had noticed it myself. I couldn't put it down just to the suspension. My mood had been all over the place, I'd been seriously depressed at times, losing my self-confidence, and getting angry for little reason.

"I know," I eventually said, very quietly. "I don't understand it either."

Paul looked straight at me.

"I think that assault has affected you somehow..."

I thought about it. He was right, of course. Obviously, the suspension was affecting me, but it didn't explain the depression or the loss of confidence in myself. And that had only happened after the assault.

"Yes, I think you're probably right," I replied, eventually.

We sat in silence, both deep in thought as it steadily grew darker outside. Eventually, Paul spoke.

"I really do understand why you want to go on fighting your suspension, although I don't know if you will win. But I really don't understand why you still want to carry on as a police officer." There was silence for several seconds before Paul continued, very quietly. "I do think you are very brave for fighting their bigotry."

"I don't feel very brave," was all I could say in response, and I meant it. I really had no choice at all but to fight what Staffordshire Police were trying to get away with, bravery wasn't part of it as I saw it. But now it was me welling up. Tears were running down my cheeks, and I felt stupid again. I covered my face. Paul pulled me close, and we knelt there hugging. It was me who spoke again, next.

"I can't explain it. I really don't feel brave at all." I was struggling to explain it or even understand it myself. "It's as if I have *got* to fight the suspension. I *cannot* let them win. I could never let them get away with it. Not even because of how important it is to win this…I just *cannot* let them win. I can't back down…if I did, it would totally destroy me!"

"Well, I still think you're being brave," Paul replied.

It was almost dark outside now. But in the caravan, it was much calmer.

"Do you want a cup of coffee?" I asked eventually.

Paul nodded. I pulled gently away from him and got up. Drawing the curtains and putting the lights on, I went to the kitchen to make two much-needed coffees.

We sat together at ease now, concerned for each other, but not speaking much. Everything which needed to be said had been. We chatted most of the evening, just as we always had done. Eventually, I got up and turned the lights off before we headed for bed.

I had difficulty getting to sleep, Paul was very quickly fast asleep. Disjointed thoughts were rushing around in my head. Eventually, I drifted into a fitful sleep.

I was being viciously kicked, blow after blow colliding with my head. I lunged out to parry the kicks – and found myself punching the headboard of the bed. Paul woke up…

"What's the matter?" he grunted, turning over, concerned.

"Nothing. No, just a nightmare. I'm all right. Really," I tried to reassure him.

I lay down, shaking, my heart pounding. That had been scary! It had seemed so real! I was almost frightened to shut my eyes but eventually calmed down enough to drift back into an uneasy sleep. I didn't want Paul to know what had just happened.

The following morning, we got up as though nothing had happened. We had breakfast and went for a long walk along the beach and scrambled onto the rocks at the end. We climbed high and then scrambled down to a small, isolated ledge facing the sea on the other side of the promontory. The waves crashing beneath only emphasised the triviality of what had happened the evening before. Wave after wave pounded relentlessly onto the rocks beneath, unseeing, and uncaring. What was happening to our lives was an insignificant event in the vastness of time, yet to us personally, it was hugely important. We sat in silence staring out to sea for a long time, the crashing waves, and the stiff breeze were calming, and I didn't want to leave. But eventually, Paul looked at his watch. It was time to go. We clambered back over the rocks to the beach and walked along side by side, each lost in our thoughts.

We journeyed back to Rugeley in almost total silence but with no tension between us. Before dropping me off Paul emphasised his support for what I was doing. But as Paul's car disappeared around the corner at the top of the road, I was left standing on the drive with my bags and a whole load of new worries. What was that all about which had so frightened me in my sleep last night? Was I going mad? The realisation that the assault was now affecting me in ways I hadn't expected left me in turmoil, yet I now had to walk into the house and face my parents.

"Hello, Steven. Did you have a good time?" asked my mother cheerfully as I walked into the lounge.

"Yes, it was nice, we really enjoyed it. Thanks for letting us use the caravan," was all I said, as I made my excuses and walked quickly through into my room at the back. How could I ever tell them what was going on inside me? I couldn't even tell them I was gay! The emotional pressure was intense, I had to get help, and fast. I had to talk to someone urgently in confidence, someone who I could trust. The only person who was immediately available was Jenny Allen, the WPC who came around to see me with the sergeant the night it all happened. Jenny had been very understanding then and I did trust her. I phoned the station, and to my relief, Jenny was on duty and was in the station. She agreed to come around straight away. I then called my friends Phil and Gill and they were happy for me to walk over there to see them, after seeing Jenny.

I couldn't get through the day being as mixed up emotionally as I was, yet having to pretend to my parents that nothing was wrong. They knew nothing, they didn't even know I was suspended from duty! Jenny visited a few minutes after I had called the station to speak to her. She was very understanding and offered her support in any way she could. She suggested that I start by speaking to the force welfare officer as soon as possible, to explain what was happening to him, and she told me to *trust him*. I agreed that I would contact him in the morning and take it from there, besides, I had to see him officially anyway. After Jenny had left, eager to avoid my parents as much as possible, I set off to walk around to Phil and Gills. I didn't know for how much longer I could hide the way I felt.

Phil and Gill, as expected, were very practical and supportive. I'd calmed down somewhat by the time I left for home. They loaned me a CD recording they had by the Gabrieli Consort and Players, called Venetian Vespers, a double CD recently released, of a recreation of a Vespers service at St Mark's Basilica as it might have been celebrated in 1643. I thanked them for the loan. They thought it might help me. I had never considered listening to any of this sort of choral music before, but classical music is what I always liked and classical CDs were my whole CD collection. When I got home I put the CD to one side as I was exhausted and went to bed soon after.

I woke up the following morning after a fitful night, still feeling mixed up emotionally, but at least with no further vivid dreams about being kicked. It was going to be almost impossible to keep up the pretence to my parents. I was still frightened and upset, and I desperately needed help, I knew I could not easily phone the force welfare officer from home, so I set off for the station. Damn it! I did not care what they said now about not going down, the worst they could do was to throw me out again. Would they stoop to that? The world seemed detached from me as I walked into town, my mind had taken as much as it could.

I soon found myself in the station yard and seconds later entered the station by the back door. I ran quickly up the back stairs, eager to avoid seeing anybody I did not have to; I couldn't hide my emotional turmoil easily. I entered the sanctuary of the sub-divisional office. Sheila, to my dismay, was not on her own, Sgt Allerton was also in the office. Their conversation stopped as I entered.

"Steve! How are you?" asked Sheila, obviously pleased to see me. I had been absent from the station for the previous month.

"I'm OK, Sheila," I lied.

"How can I help you?" she asked.

"I need to speak to Rob Williams, the force welfare officer. Have you got his phone number?" I really wanted to call Rob Williams from the station but Sgt Allerton was there, I felt extremely awkward about discussing the issue there. Sheila looked the number up and wrote it down for me on a scrap of paper. I thanked her and turned to leave. Sgt Allerton stopped me from leaving by standing in the doorway.

"Steve, it's good to see you back again. I've wanted to have a chat with you for a while, can you spare a few minutes?"

I stood for a few seconds, panicking, wondering what to do. I was not really in the mood for a chat, but, on the other hand, I had always got on well with Howard Allerton.

"Yes OK, Sarge."

I followed him out of Sheila's office and across the corridor into his tiny office buried in the depths of the building. He pulled up a chair, invited me to sit down and shut the door before sitting down behind his desk, smiling.

"I'm glad you came in, Steve, I was worried about you. You have been missed, this past month or so. How are things now?"

I was not really in the mood for this conversation, yet he was genuinely amiable and seemed concerned. I relaxed slightly, though still found it difficult to concentrate on what was happening. It was going to be exceedingly difficult to lie my way through this.

"I'm fine, Sarge," I replied, somewhat feebly.

"I know you've had a few problems at home, how is it there now?"

"No problem at all. It never really was. That was nothing. I was just worried about not having a job, that's all really, Sarge, it really was nothing."

"Have you told your parents that you're gay yet?"

"No, Sarge, I haven't yet…" I paused, not knowing what to say. This was making me angry again, it was none of their bloody business. I was being pushed into a corner.

"…Sarge, I've heard that there have been one or two problems from some people around the station who don't like the fact that I'm gay."

"Well, if anything has been said, I've not heard it, Steven. Let me reassure you about that; you are a valuable member of the team here, and you have been missed. There are a lot of people who support you around the station." He smiled reassuringly at me. His answer seemed genuine. Nevertheless, I had no reason to distrust the information I had already been given to the contrary. I was confused, I did not know where I stood any more.

"OK, Sarge, thanks." I smiled weakly at him. He looked at me for several seconds before he said anything.

"Despite what you've just told me, you don't look OK, Steven."

I could not hide it any longer, I was desperate to talk to someone and I was on the point of breaking down. I looked across at Howard Allerton, he seemed genuinely concerned, and I could trust him.

"There is a problem, Sarge. I desperately need to talk to someone…"

"You can trust me, Steve. You can speak to me confidentially."

I was being extremely stupid. The person I *really* should have been unburdening my worries to was just a phone call away on a piece of paper I was still clutching in my sweating hand!

"Thanks, Sarge…" I hesitated for a few seconds before continuing, "I've had a slight argument with my friend, Paul…"

"He's the gay friend who phoned us a month ago…"

"Yes, Sarge. We went away for the weekend, and we got back last night… We argued on Saturday night, he wants me to leave Staffordshire Police" I looked up again at Howard Allerton before continuing.

"He also told me he was worried that there was something wrong with me since that assault. He said I was acting strangely. To be honest, Sarge…" I hesitated, recalling that vivid dream. "…I have noticed my mood has changed recently."

I looked up again at Sgt Allerton, he was sitting looking at me impassively.

"How did you meet Paul?"

"I answered an advert which he put in one of the local newspapers last year. The Post or the Mercury, I cannot remember which one. That's how we met."

He nodded.

"Steve, can you trust Paul? He doesn't go sleeping around, does he?"

The question took me by surprise, I really wasn't expecting the change of direction the conversation was taking now.

"I totally trust him, Sarge!

He's very genuine." I was feeling a bit worried.

"Sarge, although we slept in the same bed at the weekend, we didn't do anything except sleep. We're just friends."

"It's OK, Steve, what you've told me is confidential. It will not get any further. I suggest you go home and make an appointment with the welfare officer."

"OK, Sarge, I'll phone him this morning."

I got up; Sgt Allerton opened the door for me.

"Try not to worry Steve, there's no problem here. Go and get yourself sorted out; we need you back down here again soon."

He held out his hand, smiling. I shook it and made my way quickly out of the station and headed home, still clutching the piece of paper.

Something was worrying me as I walked back home. Sgt Allerton was genuinely concerned though, and he did reassure me that our conversation was confidential. I was puzzled that he had not heard of any problems with other officers. I had no reason to doubt the reports I had received to the contrary. He was just trying to reassure me, trying not to worry me. I could trust him.

As soon as I got home, after making sure that I could phone without being overheard, I phoned headquarters and asked to be put through to the welfare officer, Rob Williams. The last time I had spoken to him was when he had called into the station the day after a particularly nasty fatal road accident I had been sent to when he had asked everyone who had been sent to deal with the accident if they were OK or needed any support. We had laughed that suggestion off then, the macho canteen culture taking over.

Rob was pleasant and easy to talk to and he was already aware of my situation. He arranged to come over to visit me at home on Wednesday morning, two days later. I occupied myself in the meantime. I spoke to Mike in Lichfield, Andy's friend, who was a counsellor. I arranged to go and see him at his home on Thursday evening. All this was done without my parents knowing anything about it – or of my suspension from duty, or that I was gay, but at least it was giving me a purpose, something to do, something to take my mind off things.

I remembered the Venetian Vespers CD that Phil and Gill had loaned me. I went to my downstairs room, shut the door, put the CD on, lay on the floor and shut my eyes; so many difficult and unpleasant thoughts kept going through my mind. I had to try and shut them down. But then the music started. Three chimes of a sacristy bell, then an organ Intonazione, followed by Versicle and Response, an Antiphon which was sung by a single voice and this led to Dixit Dominus by Rigatti. Ninety minutes of solo's, choir, plainchant and intricately woven polyphony. I was totally lost in the incredibly beautiful music which was filling my room and it was difficult to pull myself out of the bliss I was now experiencing, to get up to change to the second CD. After it finished, I put the first CD on again and listened right through, and yet again after that finished. It was the first time that I realised how much listening to music can help with anxiety and stress; a potent balm to soothe a painful mind. It started my love of early choral music which has never left me. Venetian Vespers was played over and over during the following weeks, I soon bought myself a copy and it remains a favourite album.

Rob Williams called round as appointed on Wednesday morning, I had vaguely told my mother that someone from the police was coming around to see me and left it at that, hoping that she would not ask further. The meeting lasted almost two hours. With relief, I realised I should have contacted him much sooner. Several people had recently been telling me to contact Rob Williams, I wished I had listened and acted on their advice sooner.

Rob Williams was very understanding and sympathetic. I really could trust him; he was completely on my side. He agreed that what my SDO and commandant had said was wrong and that they definitely shouldn't have asked me to resign. He also said that he could not see why they should not let me back on duty straight away and he would draft a report to that effect. He did point out, however, that from what he had seen and heard already, the force was putting far too much emphasis on my sexuality, he had seen reports at headquarters. It only confirmed what I already knew.

As I shut the door on Rob when he left, I felt as if a huge burden had been taken off me, and I felt much more positive. Now I had someone from headquarters who was on my side, helping me, seeing the injustice of what the force was trying to do to me. I was not surprised that reports were going around headquarters about my sexuality, but it only made me angry and more determined the bastards were not going to get away with it! Now I was in a much more positive state of mind and more importantly, I was fighting.

So far, the past three days had been quite productive. I had learnt much about anxiety and depression from phone conversations I'd made. I realised just how little I had known about it. On top of that, I had proof that the force was using my sexuality officially against me and that was a big step forward. Later the same evening I was going over to Lichfield to see Mike, someone to talk to face to face, someone else I could trust and talking helped very much.

The phone rang, it was Rob Williams.

"Hello, Steve. How are you feeling now?"

"I'm feeling much better Rob, I appreciated your visit this morning, I know now that I have someone on my side. I should have contacted you much sooner!"

"Yes, Steve. Lots of officers are reluctant to contact me, they don't think they can speak to me in confidence, and they don't trust me! Anyway, the reason I was calling was just to warn you. I have just had a conversation with a superintendent here, who is going around with a story about you that has leaked out from Rugeley. He said that you had told someone at Rugeley that you had sex with your friend Paul three times last weekend and that

159

you are now HIV positive! I did tell him that from the conversation we'd had earlier it was not true, that it obviously could not be true – no one could get a diagnosis so soon after unprotected sex. I do believe you, of course, Steve, but it shows how little you can trust some of the officers at Rugeley. Anyway, I have stopped that rumour now. I thought I ought to let you know."

I was shocked.

"Thank you, Rob, thanks for letting me know – that's kind of you. It must have been Sergeant Allerton who spread that from that conversation we had the other day, he promised me it was confidential! He's lying! I never said anything of the sort to him!"

"I know that Steve, but it just shows what sort of battle you've got now. Anyway, I'll let you know of any further developments, and I'll speak to you very soon."

I replaced the handset. That lie would be all over the bloody station now! Once again, I was incredibly angry. The conversation I'd had with Howard Allerton had been confidential! And it must have been him who spread the malicious rumour, there was no one else it could have been; what chance did I have now to sort things out? And he had blatantly *lied* if what Rob said was correct! He had seemed so welcoming and supportive and that was all a sham; that was manifestly obvious now. What were they trying to do? What were they afraid of?

I became more determined than ever now to sort things out. I was going over to Lichfield to see Mike soon and shift two was on nights, I would pop into the station to have a quiet word with Ian Gilbey on the way back.

My evening with Mike was useful. The symptoms I was

describing to him which were affecting me now – tiredness over the past few weeks, anxiety and depression could so easily and simply be explained by my sudden change in lifestyle. I was going out to clubs at least once a week, and I was tired and feeling run down because of that. Mike also agreed with my suggestion that it might also be connected to the assault as it had all really started after that.

I had a long chat with Mike about my problems with the police. He was incredibly supportive and suggested that I should speak to his friend Iain Ferguson in London; Iain was a counsellor in the same organisation, but he was also a member of the Lesbian and Gay Police Association. I agreed, indeed was eager, that Mike would pass my telephone number on to Iain as soon as possible. I said goodbye to Mike quite late in the evening feeling much calmer. Before setting off I asked Mike if I could phone Ian Gilbey to check that he was working in the control room. I did so; Ian was there so I told him I would call in on my way home.

I was worried about entering the station now, unsure of my reception. Fortunately, the station was extremely quiet when I walked in, and Ian was on his own in the control room. I slumped down in the chair next to him, just as I had done so many times in the past whilst on duty in the office, but it felt so different tonight. I was looking forward to a frank chat with Ian about what was happening. But what Ian had to tell me was not very encouraging.

Many of the officers at the station were now finding my sexuality a problem, especially now that it was all over the station that they thought my 'friend' Paul was HIV positive. Several of the officers were saying that they did not want to work with me again, including Sergeant Dave Jones, whom I had trusted and

161

worked with since joining. And Inspector Robertson had told my shift the other day, that he hated gay people. What could I do? I could not officially go to the station to set things right; they had stopped me. It was becoming very clear why my SDO and the commandant had told me not to visit the station – my suspicions were coming true.

Ian was very sympathetic, but not overly optimistic about my chances of getting back. At the very least, not for a long time.

"They're running around like headless chickens up at headquarters, they haven't got a clue what to do. It's going to be a long time before you get back down here now Steven, if at all."

"But it's not fair! They are spreading lies about me! I can do the job; I am no threat to anyone! *Damn it! I'm good at the job, what else counts!*"

Ian swivelled in his chair towards me, his frustration expressed as anger. He pointed his finger at me.

"*I* know that but try telling that to those idiots at headquarters. *That's* your problem!" he said waving his hand vaguely in the direction of Stafford. "That's where the root of your problem is. Right at the top!"

We looked at each other for several seconds, Ian looked as frustrated as I felt. Eventually, it was Ian who broke the silence.

"Changing the subject, do you remember you were going to get me a programme for Symphony Hall in Birmingham?"

"Sorry Ian, I totally forgot!"

"I'll forgive you, under the circumstances!"

"I'll drop one in for you soon, I promise."

Symphony Hall had only opened a couple of years before and I'd had several conversations previously about how wonderful the acoustics were there. Ian was interested in going. I left the station a brief time later even more despondent about the situation. My hands were tied, there was nothing I could do.

But I could do something. The following day Iain Ferguson phoned me from LAGPA, Mike had called him. I spent a long time talking to Iain and he was extremely helpful. He was audibly shocked at what had happened, he suggested it might be an idea if he contacted headquarters in Stafford and tried to smooth things out there, to point them in the right direction, so that they no longer ran around like "headless chickens". The Metropolitan Police in London were used to sorting out these issues, it was not a problem there.

As the days passed by, I became ever more frustrated at the lack of action. All the time I was away from the station, the more people there were turning against me. It was the end of May now and I had been informed that they would review my situation then, although I doubted that I would get back so soon. Rob Williams had drafted a report saying that there was no reason for me not to resume duties, so from now on they would have to be much more blatant about their real reason for not letting me go back.

I managed to speak to Paul. I told him about my conversation with Sgt Allerton and the later lies he had then spun to headquarters. I tried to emphasise that they did not know who he was; Paul was just a name to them. Paul took it better than I'd feared and was understandably as annoyed and frustrated as I was.

As the end of May came and then passed, and I still had heard nothing from the station, I decided to phone Rob Rawles one evening. I was feeling much more positive, and more determined than I had. Rob was very pleasant and polite when I first phoned him, but that soon changed.

"I've seen the force welfare officer as you asked; he said that

163

he had no objection to me resuming duties, he said that there was nothing wrong with me…"

"He might have done, Steven, but you can't start back until you are told to, officially. I've been instructed to tell you that you will not be allowed back on duty until you submit the result of an HIV test to the police surgeon."

My anger rose quickly, so this was their next trick!

"So, I'm still suspended then?"

"No, you're not suspended! You're just not allowed back until you're told otherwise, and until you submit that report to the police surgeon, is that clear?"

"Yes, it is. I'm still suspended!"

There was an uneasy silence, I was angry.

"Anyway, Rob, I *am* aware of the problems down at the station, I have spoken to officers there and Rob Williams has told me that he knows there is a problem. I know what some officers have been saying."

"Really, Steven? I haven't heard anything."

"You're lying to me. There *are* problems and you know it, or it's obviously a problem for you if you haven't heard about them, whatever you may, or may not have heard!"

Another silence before I continued.

"And, just to let you know. I have contacted a member of the Lesbian and Gay Police Association in London, and he is concerned. They are aware of these problems and are helping to sort them out."

"Really! I do not think that was a clever idea. There was no need to contact anybody outside the force!"

Rob was angry at that; I guessed he would be.

"I don't suppose you do, but I'm sure, for my part, it was a good idea."

He got the message and changed the subject quickly.

"Steven, I am glad you called, because there's a court warning come through and you're one of the witnesses. It is at Rugeley Magistrates Court, at the usual time on the ninth of June. Make sure you wear your uniform for that."

"So, I'm considered well enough to attend court then?"

He did not answer it.

"Anyway, I'll let you know of any further developments as they arise."

"I hope you do."

I replaced the handset. Not once had the bastard asked how I was, considering I was still 'suspended' on sick leave. It showed their real intention. And now I had to give the police surgeon the result of an HIV test!

I thought about it. I was certain that they could not insist on that, that if they tried to, they were breaking the law. I phoned Mike in Lichfield and Iain Ferguson from LAGPA to check, and they both agreed that no one could make me give the result of an HIV test. In the meantime, I was still suspended.

A couple of days later I had another call from Rob Williams at headquarters.

"Steve! I am just phoning to let you know that I have heard, on the grapevine, that you are going to be summoned to see a superintendent here at headquarters very soon. I do not know what they want to see you about, but do not give in, we'll get you back on duty somehow."

What did they want to see me for? By now I did not trust them, and I was worried. But then again, by going directly to headquarters, the very place this awful situation had started from, I might be able to sort this mess out properly and finally.

I was losing my patience with the delays in getting me back

on duty, it was now early June, and every day which went by only increased the worry and the pressure to sort out the problems there. I refused to be intimidated by being told I had to stay away from the station, and I remembered that Ian Gilbey had asked me to get him a programme for Symphony Hall in Birmingham; it would give me the perfect excuse to call in if anyone challenged me. Anyway, I had often called in to see colleagues when I was off duty, as did most of the other officers. They would have to be bloody blatant with it if they said anything.

The following afternoon I walked down to the station, it was a warm and sunny day, it was almost summer now and I didn't need my jacket for once! And I was quite relaxed and in a positive mood – just let them dare to challenge me!

I walked into the station, and there were one or two officers about, but otherwise, it was quiet and relaxed. Ian was in the control room. I pulled the chair up again and sat down next to him. Sergeant Jones walked into the control room; I became very conscious of him standing behind me. I turned and said, "Good afternoon" wondering how he would react after what Ian had told me about him, but he was polite and in a reasonable mood.

I gave Ian the leaflet and we talked about Symphony Hall; I had been several times since it had been opened. The phone rang and stopped our conversation. I sat and waited, swivelling in my chair, it felt good to be back in the control room!

Sergeant Jones had gone again to my relief. After what Ian had told me, I did not much feel like holding a conversation with him while I was still suspended. The other phone rang, Ian was still talking on the other line, so I picked up the telephone. It was an easy enquiry, and a few seconds later I put the phone down again.

Ian was a long time on the other line! I gathered there was

an imminent job for someone, from the notes he was taking. It was as if I was back on duty; it was a good feeling. The bell rang, and there was someone at the enquiry desk now. I looked around, but no one else was in the office so I went through. Again, a simple and easy job, a young man producing his driving documents for inspection. I took his documents off him and walked back into the office. Ian was still on the phone, although he was finishing the conversation. He put the receiver down and was about to pick up the radio transmitter.

"Ian, sorry to interrupt, but someone's producing, what shall I do?"

"Oh, I'm a bit busy, I'm just sending one of the patrols to a job, can you fill in the form and I'll sign it being as technically you're not on duty."

That is what I expected him to say, but I wanted him to say it! I would have to go after this, even if we had not finished our conversation. I had to get back home, although I was enjoying being back! Whilst Ian was sending a patrol to the job I pulled out the book and began transferring the details from the driving documents. Sergeant Jones walked back into the office, picked up a file and walked straight back out. I finished filling in the form and left it on the desk next to Ian for him to sign. He put the transmitter down and turned towards me. At last, we might be able to finish our conversation!

Sergeant Jones walked back into the office, he looked serious.

"Steven, the Inspector would like to see you in his office straight away, can you go down please."

I looked at Ian, he looked puzzled too. What did he want? Considering his views, I could not imagine he wanted a cosy chat. It might be that he felt it necessary to enquire about my welfare, so far there had been a marked absence of such concern considering I was supposed to be suspended on sick leave. I walked down to his office and knocked on the door.

"Come in."

I opened the door and stepped inside; the Inspector was sitting behind his desk looking serious. This was the first time I had spoken to him since that cosy welcoming chat in the corridor after the parade, all those weeks ago.

"Yes sir?" I inquired.

"Sergeant Jones informs me that you have been in the control room dealing with members of the public."

"Yes sir, I only answered a call and took some driving documents to fill in while Ian was busy, I only called in to…"

The inspector cut me short,

"You shouldn't be in there dealing with members of the public dressed the way you are, do not do it again in my station!"

His voice was raised and intimidating, I was shocked but knew I had to stay in control, so I stared at him impassively. What was wrong with what I had done? Many officers dealt with members of the public in civilian clothes! Damn it, we have a civilian controller at times, and anyway, I am dressed smartly, I thought, as the inspector continued, not giving me a chance to reply or say anything.

"Anyway, you should not be down here at all now, you've been told to stay away from the station until you hear otherwise! What would happen if there was an incident at the station while you were here? What would you do? *You are a health risk!*" he bellowed at me, his face turning red, banging his fist hard down on his desk, "I do not want to see you back in here until you're told otherwise, now *get out of my station!*" he shouted so loudly it made me jump and such that anyone in the station would hear.

There were a few moments of total silence. We stared into each other's eyes, a mutual hatred burning through the space between us. I was shaking, and my anger was near to exploding, I concentrated on my stare, and I hoped the message was getting through.

"By the way, Mr Johnson, I've been instructed to inform you that Superintendent Layton wants to see you at headquarters at four o'clock next Thursday the tenth of June. Go along and see what he has to say to you. Now *get out of my station.*" He spat that out with so much loathing.

The contempt that the bastard sitting on the other side of the desk was showing towards me was nothing to match the contempt that I now held him in.

"I *will* be back, *sir,*" was all I said, very calmly but very firmly.

I stared at him for several more seconds before turning and walking quietly out of the office and closing the door with a very restrained quiet click. My control was near breaking point now. I walked quickly down the corridor, physically pushing past Sergeant Jones who was walking back towards the inspector's office, no doubt to gloat after the roasting I had just suffered. He was the bastard who went and told the inspector I was in the station. I left the station by the back door which slammed hard shut behind me. I made sure it did.

I was angry. I had never, ever felt anger like this, I could have easily committed a murder, it was frightening me. Tears were streaming down my face, uncontrollably and everything was a blur as I ran home, not even stopping to check for traffic as I crossed the roads. Faster and faster, I ran, further and further away from the station I now hated. How could I ever get back there now with an officer in charge who could treat me like that? *I was a health risk!* It was blatantly obvious what he was referring to!

The further I ran the angrier I became, in no time at all I was on our road, then running down the drive and into the house. My mother looked at me shocked at what she saw.

"Steven, what's the matter?"

I could not calm down enough to talk, so I pushed past her and ran through my room into the back garden, and she followed me through.

"Steven, *what's the matter?*" she asked more emphatically, looking very frightened. I could hide it no longer, and it all came spilling out.

"I'm so sorry, Mum, it's that bloody new inspector in charge of the station…he's just kicked me out, told me to get out of *his* station! I'm suspended from duty, that's why I haven't been going down there for the past few weeks, they suspended me!" I was shouting, walking round and round the garden to try and get rid of the adrenaline, tears were still streaming down my face. My mother was following me around, trying to grab me and stop me.

"Why, Steven? Steven! Please, Steven! But why have they suspended you?" She looked worried and frightened.

"Because they found out about me; they know about me and Paul. I told them months ago and now they're trying to get rid of me – because I'm gay!"

My mother took hold of me, I was crying uncontrollably now and collapsed onto her shoulder, and she hugged me so tight; that was so reassuring, I needed my mum.

"I know you are Steven, and I've known for a long time. It's not a problem at all. But what *they* are doing to you is! That's disgusting! After all the work you've done for them!"

My mother squeezed me tightly and I was safe, she calmed me down, and her support was so much needed. She took a huge burden off my shoulders.

Chapter 9

Fighting the Establishment

"They're trying to get rid of me." That had been the first time I had said it. They did not want me back at all, they wanted me to go. From what Ian Gilbey had told me, they hadn't got a clue how to manage the problem at headquarters, so the most obvious thing to do was to get rid of the problem altogether. It was becoming increasingly clear that I was going to have to fight extremely hard to get back at all.

The pressure had been building steadily for weeks until it had become unbearable, but now that my parents knew, a huge burden had been lifted. They had no problem accepting me being gay and they gave me their full support. It made my position so much easier because now I did not have to hide anything, I did not have to worry about them asking awkward questions and I could concentrate on the fight I had ahead of me.

I needed some immediate help; advice on what rights I had, and what I might be able to do. I phoned the local Citizen's Advice Bureau and made an appointment for the following Monday morning. The more organisations who knew what was happening, the better the chance of sorting it all out properly I now realised. The police did not like any adverse publicity, I already knew that they would do anything to avoid any damaging revelations.

The CAB offices were in the council buildings, right

171

opposite the police station, something I noticed with a wry smile. I walked into them wondering if anybody, particularly the inspector, would notice me – almost wanting, willing him to see me. As I discussed my predicament with one of their advisors, I could see the inspector's office through the window in the interview room we used. If only he knew what we were discussing!

The meeting with the CAB was useful, for one thing, it was pointed out to me that even though I was a special constable, I was still classed as an employee and had the same rights as a paid employee. We decided that the CAB would write to Staffordshire Police Headquarters to find out whether sexual orientation was included in their equal opportunities policy, but I knew it wasn't. It would also send a clear message to headquarters that I was not going to give in. I mentioned my forthcoming meeting with Superintendent Layton at headquarters, but we agreed it would be better for me to go along, initially, to see what sort of line they were going to take, but the thought of the impending meeting was worrying me.

Before leaving, the advisor I saw made a passing comment that it might have solved a lot of problems if there had been a gay switchboard or support group somewhere locally that I could have contacted for support, help or advice. I agreed with her, especially if there had been local. I made another appointment at the CAB the following week, to discuss the outcome of the forthcoming meeting at headquarters and left the building a lot happier, I hoped the inspector had seen me leaving. I set off for home still thinking about the idea of a local support group.

The most immediate issue which was worrying me was my court appearance on Wednesday morning. It was not that I was afraid of giving evidence in court, I had done that plenty of times before, but this would be the first time I had been back at the station in uniform and on duty for a couple of months and the climate there concerning me was quite different now.

I was extremely anxious and nervous as I changed into my uniform and set off for the station, yet I need not have worried. The inspector was not around to my relief. I met the other three officers in the parade room, and we set off from the station a few minutes later. We spent an hour or two sitting around in the custody area at the back of the courtrooms, waiting for the trial to begin. I was relieved and surprised by the level of support given to me; my suspension was discussed, and they all gave me their backing for what I was standing up for and were disgusted at the way I was being treated. That was genuine and it pleased me.

The trial was called off when the defendant did not turn up, and we were all dismissed. It had been a wasted morning. Yet, no, it had not. I had picked up some much-needed support from my colleagues. I now realised that the problem was not universal, it was only from a handful of officers. Unfortunately for me, that included two sergeants and the officer in charge of the station, and I knew that the longer all this went on the worse it would get. I returned home frustrated but much more positive. Frustrated because I had just effectively been on duty, and I could see no way that they could now stop me from resuming normal duties. Hopefully, my meeting at headquarters the following afternoon would sort it all out.

The following afternoon I drove over to headquarters nervous but eager to walk away afterwards with a positive result. I parked the car and walked over to the main administration building, the last time I had been there was the day I had my application interview.

I buzzed reception and they let me in. I sat in the foyer, nervously thumbing through a magazine, for all the world it was just like waiting for my turn to see the dentist! I did not know the officer who I had to see, I glanced around every time someone walked past, wondering when they would come for me.

Eventually, ten long minutes later, someone walked over and asked me to follow them. We walked over to a door just behind, next to reception. I was shown into the small office and introduced to Superintendent Layton who was sitting looking serious behind a desk, and an inspector sitting alongside the desk.

"Thank you for coming, Mr Johnson, please take a seat." said the superintendent.

I sat down on the chair provided, several feet away from the desk the superintendent was sitting behind, this all seemed alarmingly formal. Curiously, I was extremely calm and collected. I had to present myself well and I knew I was in the right; Staffordshire Police were very much in the wrong.

The superintendent opened a file lying on the desk in front of him and scanned the papers inside.

"Well, Mr Johnson, I see from your file that you have an excellent record, there are some letters of commendation for the work you've done, you've given a lot of your time to help us and worked very professionally…until now." He looked up from the papers and stared at me.

Alarm bells started ringing inside me, it had all seemed quite positive until that last statement which sounded ominous. I stayed calm, just a slightly puzzled expression on my face.

"What do you mean, sir?" I replied, quietly.

"I see that a friend of yours, Paul, phoned the police a few weeks ago because he was concerned for your state of mind, which is why we wanted to see you today."

"That was all a big mistake," I quickly replied, "Paul had overreacted to the situation, I was not suicidal. I was just depressed about my lack of a *paid job*." I emphasised that point, not sure whether the irony and subtlety of it would be recognised, it did not seem to be.

"Nevertheless," continued the superintendent, "we considered it wise to give you a few weeks off active duties and then to review the situation, which is what I am doing now."

"There is nothing wrong with me, sir. The force welfare officer came out to see me a couple of weeks ago and he agreed that I was OK, he told me he could not see any reason why I shouldn't resume duties straight away."

The superintendent shuffled through to a piece of paper further down, obviously the report from Rob Williams.

"Yes, I've seen that, and that's what we're here to decide." He spent a few seconds scanning through it, and there was an uneasy silence. The superintendent looked up again. He could not keep playing that game, we all knew that my suspension had nothing to do with my state of mind, so I decided to change tack.

"I am aware, sir, that there have been one or two problems at the station since I came out that I am gay; it seems obvious to me that it's *that* fact that is the real reason that I've been suspended."

It hit home, and the expression on the superintendent's face suddenly hardened.

"You are not suspended, Mr Johnson. You have been told not to go on duty until told otherwise, that's all." His voice was cold and hard.

"That sounds like suspension to me," I replied, slightly more abruptly, my anger was rising, but I had to remain calm.

"What problems are you referring to?" asked the

175

superintendent.

"Well sir, when my SDO and the divisional commandant came around to see me at home when I was *suspended*, they made it very plain that they wanted me to resign or to transfer to another station because other officers at Rugeley might find my sexuality a problem. I have been told by several officers from Rugeley that some of the officers there are finding my sexuality a problem, they include Sergeant Jones, Sergeant Allerton and Inspector Robertson."

I paused, waiting for a response but both officers looked on impassively, so I continued, "I was told that Inspector Robertson openly told shift two on parade one day that he hated gay people when he knew about me and that I worked with shift two mostly. Then when I visited the station last week to see Ian Gilbey, the controller, I was called into Inspector Robertson's office where he shouted me out of the station. He said I was a health risk, sir, and he shouted at me to get out of his station."

The superintendent pulled out a typed sheet and held it up.

"Yes, Inspector Robertson has sent me a report about that incident."

The bastard! They were doing everything they could to discredit me!

"On top of that, sir, I had a confidential conversation with Sergeant Allerton at the station a couple of weeks ago when I told him about my anxiety and depression since that assault. I was told it was a confidential conversation, but I had a phone call from the force welfare officer a few days afterwards and he told me that a senior officer here at headquarters was going around saying that I had slept with Paul three times the week before and had unprotected sex with him and I was now HIV positive. Everyone at the station has heard it now, and it's not true, he is

176

lying, I never said anything like that!"

Superintendent Layton pulled out another typed report.

"Yes, Mr Johnson, Sergeant Allerton has sent us a report of that conversation you had with him." He held up the report, it was two or three pages long. That two-faced bastard Allerton, I thought to myself.

"Are you saying that some of the things he has said are not true?"

"It seems that way from what I've heard, sir," I replied, controlling my anger.

"Do you want me to read it out to you, Mr Johnson?"

"Yes."

The superintendent began reading from the report. It began quite accurately, but then it diverged right away from what I had said.

"...and then Mr Johnson told me that to reassure his friend Paul that he still cared about him and loved him that he slept with Paul that night and he had unprotected anal sex with him, which had happened on numerous occasions before including after he had found out that Paul was HIV positive. Mr Johnson told me that he met Paul through a 'contact' magazine..."

The superintendent finished reading the report and looked up at me with a look of disgust.

"Would you tell me what in that report is not accurate, Mr Johnson?"

"The part where he says I had unprotected anal sex with Paul, that Paul is HIV positive and that I met Paul through a contact magazine. They are lies, I never said anything of the sort, and they are not true!"

"You're saying that Sergeant Allerton is lying in this report?" He waved it in front of me.

"Yes! Absolutely! Do you honestly think, even if it were true, that I would tell Sergeant Allerton *that*?"

The Superintendent stared at me for several seconds, there was an uneasy silence, and it was making me nervous; this whole meeting was rapidly degenerating into nothing short of an interrogation. Sheer panic was rising inside me, my hands were sweaty and trembling. I tried extremely hard to remain as calm as possible.

"Mr Johnson, do you think that you have been the subject of victimisation?"

"Oh yes, definitely! Yes!" I sat bolt upright.

There was another uneasy silence.

"Would you mind telling me what sort of sexual activity you get up to with Paul then?"

I could not believe what I was hearing, panic was clawing at my throat, I was frightened, this was unreal, it could not be happening to me! I had to stay in control. He had no right to expect an answer to that.

"That is none of your business," I said eventually, very calmly.

The superintendent had picked up a pen which was hovering over a notepad. He was desperate for anything to discredit me and get rid of me, that much was obvious now.

"Have you ever had anal sex with Paul then?"

"That is none of your business, I refuse to answer that, anyway I have already told you!"

"Are you going out with this Paul?"

"No, like I said to Sergeant Allerton and which he put in that report, Paul is now going out with Gary, but we are still friends."

"How did you meet Paul then?"

"I met him through a personal advertisement in one of the

local papers, I do not remember which one, it was the Post or the Mercury. It was not through a contact magazine, whatever one of those is."

The superintendent was writing on the notepad.

"You said the Post or the Mercury…what are they?"

"They're the local free newspapers which come through the door every week They're quite normal, there's nothing wrong with them!" my voice was raised slightly, out of incredulity that he did not know what I was referring to. I could see the superintendent writing 'Post or Mercury' on the notepad. He looked up again, the pen hovering, waiting for more 'incriminating' information.

"So, Mr Johnson, this friend of Paul, Gary, who is he?"

I was becoming ever more worried at the way the meeting was going, it was clear now that this was just an exercise to get as much information about my gay friends as possible and to find anything to incriminate me or discredit me, that would give them an excuse to get rid of me. I did not know what to say, but the Superintendent's tone was becoming harder and more threatening.

"Gary is Paul's boyfriend," I answered eventually.

"So, Paul and Gary are going out with each other?"

"Yes, I just told you that! Paul and I are just friends."

I instantly regretted saying even that. What right did Staffordshire Police have to interrogate me about my friends, there was no suggestion of any illegal activity! I was being treated like a criminal just because I was gay!

"How did Paul and Gary meet each other?"

It was clear now that this meeting was nothing less than an interrogation to try and find something they could use against me. I would give them no further information, and I would stick by it. I calmed down slightly and sat in the chair, relaxed, but my palms were still sweating.

"I do not know, but anyway, that is none of your business."

The superintendent looked agitated, his temper was rising, and I became scared.

"Do Paul and Gary live together?"

"I'm not answering that, it's none of your business."

"What is Paul's surname then?"

I remained silent, the superintendent's voice was raised and angry.

"Please tell us Gary's surname then."

I sat as still as possible, deliberately smiling slightly, trying to keep myself as calm as I could, and said nothing.

"Where do they work?"

My fear was rising, but I had to remain in control of this. My mind was frantically trying to work out if I bolted suddenly before they could get to me, how many seconds it would take to get out of the building, run to my car and drive out. If they made any move towards me, I would bolt. My focus turned back to the superintendent.

"Where do they live then?" asked the superintendent.

"As I said, that is none of your business, no one has a right to demand that sort of information when no one has done anything wrong!" I replied eventually.

The Superintendent stared at me icily, his tone was angry, and he was close to shouting.

"Mr Johnson, you should know that it is my duty to report to the chief constable as to whether you are a responsible enough person to continue serving as a police officer in this force, and at the moment I do not consider that you are!" he barked.

I glared back at him, just as icily. My voice was calm and

clear, I was absolutely in the right.

"I am demonstrating my sense of responsibility to you by refusing to answer questions to which you have no right to expect an answer," I replied, slowly and deliberately. I was more certain than ever that this could turn physical, but I tried to remain in control.

My reply was ignored, and the superintendent continued in the same vein.

"How many more gay friends do you have?"

I remained silent.

"What sort of sexual activity do Paul and Gary get up to?" he asked bluntly.

"That is none of *my* business, let alone any of *yours!*"

"Do they have a sexual relationship?"

"Would you mind telling me what sort of..."

"Mr JOHNSON!" the Superintendent barked, cutting me short, "I must remind you that if you continue to refuse to answer these questions, I will not be able to report to the executive officers that you are responsible enough to continue serving as a special constable in this force!"

I had been about to ask the superintendent if he'd like to tell me what sort of sexual activity he got up to. My heart was almost pounding in my throat now, yet there was no way I was going to answer, I was certain of that now, but my fear and anger were coming to the surface. I HAD to remain in control. I calmed down and concentrated on controlling my breathing and shaking.

"As I have already pointed out to you, I consider I am displaying my responsibility by *not* answering those questions," I thought about what pressure I might put on them before carrying on,

"...You should know that I have already contacted the

181

Lesbian and Gay Police Association and I have spoken to the Citizens Advice Bureau about these matters and about the way Staffordshire Police have treated me so far. They would like to know if sexual orientation is in the force's equal opportunities policy?"

"DO NOT THREATEN ME!" barked the superintendent.

All my muscles tensed; I was getting ready to bolt.

"I wasn't" was all I replied.

There was an uneasy hiatus. I was feeling distinctly uncomfortable, I was frightened that they would resort to beating me up in a minute to force the information they wanted from me. Bolting was looking like a definite possibility. The other inspector who was sitting in, sat impassively, silently staring at me and nodding approval to the superintendent's outbursts, he was unsettling me. I could see the lawns and the main road beyond it from the window behind the superintendent. It seemed unreal that this was happening while everyday life was going on outside; I felt trapped, I felt like a prisoner. With the hiatus still holding, it was me who spoke next.

"I'm not making threats; I was merely pointing out to you what steps I have taken to help Staffordshire Police come to the right conclusion..." I answered eventually, looking back at the superintendent.

"I can assure you, Mr Johnson,..." said the superintendent, after he had calmed down slightly, but I cut in, desperate to get the upper hand.

"When I joined Staffordshire Police I stood up in court and took an oath, that I would treat everyone I dealt with professionally without favour or affection, malice or ill-will, and what I have always taken that oath to mean is that when I am on duty, I treat *everyone* I deal with the same. I always have. I have proved my ability to police properly. Everyone. The same." I stared straight at the superintendent, waiting to see how he could wriggle out of that one. He stared back at me for several seconds, and for the first time, I could see he was feeling the pressure from me. This was developing into a battle of wills. Eventually, he spoke.

"As I was saying until you interrupted, I can assure you Staffordshire Police is an equal opportunities employer, but sexual orientation is *not* in our equal opportunities policy." He emphasised the 'not' and lingered on it.

"What is more, I do not think you have been treated badly, I think the incidents you described are perfectly understandable and reasonable responses to your homosexuality. *"YOU'RE RAMMING IT DOWN OUR THROATS!"* he shouted.

My temper flared at this statement, but I controlled it, just.

"I do not consider the lies that have been told about me and the way I was treated by the inspector to be reasonable in any way," I replied, continuing calmly, "and on the contrary, it isn't me who has been ramming my homosexuality down anybody's throats, I haven't made an issue out of it, it is Staffordshire Police who are making it an issue for me with their bigotry. I just want to get the whole *damned* thing sorted out properly and, I am *not* making an issue out of it!"

"You're being obstinate, Mr Johnson!"

"I absolutely agree!" I retorted, "On this issue I am. For once I agree with you."

The superintendent looked at the inspector. He obviously realised he was not getting anywhere.

"Well, I've got to report to the executive officers now about whether you should be allowed back on duty. Until you hear otherwise, you are to remain off duty, do you understand?"

"I certainly do, sir. I'm still suspended."

"You are not suspended at all!" barked the superintendent. I did not answer.

"That's all for now, Mr Johnson, we'll be in touch." The superintendent stood up. I was about to get up, but there was something else I wanted to say.

"I just want to point out that I am not the side in this dispute wanting any confrontation, I just want to get this problem sorted out correctly, nothing more. I am not the one making an issue out of it."

I stood up, relieved it was over. The superintendent stopped me as I walked quickly towards the door behind me.

"By the way Mr Johnson, this meeting was confidential, you should speak to nobody about what we have discussed here today, is that clear?"

I turned back towards the superintendent. I wanted to reply, I opened my mouth to reply, but I could not be bothered, I just wanted to get out. I stared at the superintendent for several seconds; did he expect me to keep quiet about what had just happened? I turned, shaking my head as I did, and walked out of the room pulling the door shut behind me, with a huge amount of relief.

I turned towards reception and freedom, my legs were shaking as I walked as quickly as I could out of the building and round to the car park. Somehow, I knew that it was not over, I was expecting them to be waiting for me or to follow me out of the car park, I would not put anything past them now. It was with a sense of urgency to get as far away from the place as possible that I drove out of headquarters and headed for home at a reckless speed. I slowed down through Cannock Chase, the emptiness and quiet of the forest was a welcome tonic to the interrogation which

I still found difficult to believe I had just endured.

I had so much anger and frustration boiling up within me that I knew I had to find an outlet for it. I was now shocked at the way I was being treated, just as if I were a criminal or worse, just because I happened to be gay. And frustration too; intense frustration now, that I could not do anything about it, I was still banned from returning to the station. Far from resolving the situation, the meeting at headquarters had only shown how deeply entrenched was their bigotry and homophobia and how officially it was expressed and at such a high level within the force, probably right to the very top, to the chief constable.

I now had so much time on my hands that I was forced into idleness. I had to find some way of channelling all the frustration and anger before it destroyed me. As for not speaking to anyone about what had just happened, I was determined now to speak to as many people as I could. It was obvious that the force was not going to sort this out properly without some sort of pressure from outside.

I phoned Iain Ferguson and told him about the interrogation; he was very concerned. I phoned the CAB again and asked to speak to someone there urgently. They asked me to go down straight away.

Cath met me at the CAB offices and took me through to the interview room again. She explained she was taking the case over; she was the manager of the branch. I explained to her the worrying series of events which had happened since my last visit. Her concern and support were extremely welcome. Again, it was suggested that it would have been especially useful if there had been a gay support group or helpline I could have phoned. I agreed and Cathy suggested that I should think about creating one myself as there certainly seemed to be a need for one locally.

It was a promising idea, but how would I go about setting it up, and what about the funding? Cathy looked thoughtful for a few seconds and then said to leave it with her, she would see whether it might be possible for us to use their facilities at the CAB offices. We agreed that I would go and discuss it with my friends and call in again the following week.

I left the office with a new sense of purpose. This was what I needed to channel all the anger and energy into. It would achieve something positive instead of destroying me. As I stepped out of the council offices and looked across to the police station opposite, I smiled. It would be ironic if I got this support group set up here, right under the nose of the inspector sitting in his office opposite!

All my gay friends, including Paul, Gary and Andy gave me much-needed support. Once again Paul could not understand why I did not just give in and resign, but I knew that was impossible. I could not give in, why should I? It would send out a clear message that the force could get away with treating anyone gay in the same way and that was utterly unacceptable. By fighting this and sticking it out, I would be sending a quite different but equally clear message. There was no way I would even consider resigning.

In the meantime, I told everyone what I had discussed with Cathy at the CAB. There was a unanimous agreement that creating a group locally would be good for the area. There would be a lot of problems to overcome, but if Cathy could negotiate the use of their offices and facilities, then I could not see why we shouldn't succeed. And it would give me something to do. I was getting quite excited already, it was somewhere to channel all my frustration and anger.

We decided that it might be good to talk to Mike in Lichfield about our proposal, he already worked for a helpline and counselling service in Birmingham, and he could be extremely useful. Mike was indeed very keen to get involved. We agreed to meet one evening when we were all free the following week.

I turned my attention back to my current predicament. There was an organisation which had recently been formed, a sort of union for special constables, our equivalent of the Police Federation. I wondered whether they would be able to help. The only trouble I had was that I did not know how to contact them. I phoned the editor of Special Beat magazine and explained why I urgently needed to speak to someone from the National Association of Special Constabulary Officers. He gave me direct contact with their president, Bill Piercy. I phoned Bill and explained my predicament. As with everyone I had turned to, he was shocked at the extent of my problems. He said he would contact the Home Office on my behalf.

I managed to find and contact a firm of solicitors in central Birmingham who represented police officers on behalf of the Police Federation and one of their solicitors agreed to see me the following Tuesday morning.

I visited the CAB again and spoke to Cathy; she was eager to find out what my friends thought of her suggestion. To my huge surprise, Cathy said that there was no objection from their side and that everyone there thought it was a positive move in the right direction and would give it their full support. I left the office delighted and in a particularly good mood. I almost felt like walking into the station opposite, straight into the inspector's office and telling him exactly what, as a direct result of the way he and his colleagues were treating me, we were about to create. Right opposite his office window!

I returned home eager to see Andy and to speak to Paul,

Gary, and Mike. Later that afternoon I actually had more news for them. A section officer in the specials from Codsall, a station a few miles from Rugeley, phoned to offer his support. Bill Piercy from NASCO contacted him directly and asked him to liaise with me. He was able to tell me that Bill Piercy was so concerned that he had already contacted the Home Office about my problems. To add to that, Iain Ferguson from LAGPA phoned later to say that he had personally already raised the issue with the Home Office a day or two earlier.

The following Tuesday morning I drove into Birmingham and found the offices of the firm of solicitors who were taking on my case, near Victoria Square in the heart of the city centre. I spent over two hours outlining the events and we agreed that they would write to my chief Constable about the issue. I left the office very satisfied. Now the bastards at headquarters would get a strong message that I was not going to crawl away whimpering.

Only a few months ago I was quietly going about my own business, working hard in the specials, and hiding from everyone that I was gay. Now suddenly I was being discussed at the Home Office. The issue had taken on quite a different scale. I was on a roller coaster ride; it was both exhilarating but also frightening. Any trace of depression or unhappiness had vanished, and I could not have been in a more positive and determined mood.

Chapter 10

False Hopes

The battle had begun; Staffordshire Police had pulled out their big guns, but now, so had I.

The interrogation at headquarters had been a pivotal event. Until that time, I had not been sure just how officially and how far up the chain of command my problems were coming from. Right from the early days when my SDO and the commandant had suspended me and put pressure on me to resign, I thought they had been instructed by someone higher, but I could not be certain. Now I knew it was from the very top – it was confirmed by a phone conversation with the force welfare officer. That knowledge only served to make me more determined than ever to win.

Bill Piercy, the President of NASCO phoned a few days later to let me know that the Home Office had passed my problem on to their equal opportunities department. A couple of days later Iain Ferguson called me asking for my permission to raise my problems at a LAGPA committee meeting, he was genuinely concerned and told me that my case was one of the most protracted and difficult they had ever dealt with. I then received a letter from my solicitor with a copy of the letter they had sent to my chief constable. Everything was moving forward steadily, and as the force was putting more pressure on me, I reciprocated by piling the pressure on them. Who would give in? It was not going to be me.

There was still an issue which was concerning me. I had always assumed that Steve Smith, my friend in the specials, had taken the fact that I was gay very well. Yet increasingly now, whenever I phoned him, he was always busy or had some excuse for not going out for a drink. The only conclusion that I could reach was that he was having difficulties associating himself with me, just like Toby had because I was gay. There was nothing I could do about it, but it only served to highlight just how cut off I now was from the former police life I'd had, and it pushed me even more towards my gay friends.

I could do nothing more but wait. In other circumstances that would have been unbearable, but I now had something to occupy my time with and to channel the anger. I had dived headfirst into the complexities and problems of setting up the new support group. More than anyone else I had the time to give it my full attention.

At the end of June, we all met at the pub in Lichfield as arranged. Nothing much of any substance was achieved that evening, but we did eventually arrive at a name for the new group. Several were discussed and turned down including the South Staffordshire Lesbian and Gay Group, but someone pointed out that SSLAG was not a promising idea, it did not convey the right impression! We eventually agreed on South Staffs Friends. We all unanimously agreed that the group should aim to supply a support and information service through the phone line generously offered to us by the CAB, and we would try and run it one evening, initially, every week.

It was obvious that somehow, we would need to find more volunteers to help on the switchboard. The best way to find people for that would be to advertise in the local press. I agreed to speak to all the local papers and try to 'sell' the story to them as a news item, that way we would get our publicity for free. Having decided that I would act as a press officer for the group, I was quick to point out that in no way was I willing to mention my problems with the police. That would be counterproductive to my fight to get back on duty at this stage. Neither was I prepared to come out to that extent. What would be the reaction of the population and criminals I knew and dealt with professionally? We all also agreed that it would be difficult to sell the group if a serving police officer were linked to it. I agreed to speak to Cathy at the CAB and see whether we could use them as a point of contact for the press, then, if I only used my first name, my anonymity would be guaranteed.

Assuming we got enough people volunteering to help we realised we would also need somewhere we could meet socially and regularly. I did not know what to suggest. The obvious solution was a room at a friendly pub somewhere in the area which we could rent out once every week or so, but I wasn't optimistic that I could find anything in or around Rugeley. If we had been in a large city, we would have had a chance. But Rugeley, a small working-class town with a reputation for trouble seemed out of the question. That was something to sort out in the future.

In the meantime, we arranged another meeting for the following week to sort out the constitution and running of the group, and a timetable to set it up. As we left the meeting that night, I felt we had already achieved something worthwhile. South Staffs Friends was effectively in existence. And I was slowly building up a close circle of gay friends, and that at least was some compensation for the life I had been cut off from.

I spoke to Cathy again and told her what we had achieved.

She had arranged that we could use their offices every Wednesday evening. I also mentioned we needed somewhere to meet and to my surprise, she thought she might know of a pub; she would make enquiries.

The following week we all met again. By the end of the evening, we had a much clearer idea of where we were going, I agreed to work with Paul and design a logo and publicity leaflets for the group on his computer. Graphic designing on Paul's PC, effectively doing what I had been professionally trained to do, was the first experience I had of creating graphics on a computer and it was a revelation! Finally, I had found a way to continue with my graphics and enjoy doing it, although I didn't realise that at the time.

We all met again in mid-July and by the end of the meeting we had sorted out most of the issues and South Staffs Friends was set on a course to start soon. As a provisional timetable, I would start speaking to the press and from now on, depending on the response, we would hold weekly meetings to get the switchboard up and running by the first Wednesday in September. By unanimous agreement, I was elected to be the chair of South Staffs Friends.

In all the excitement of getting South Staffs Friends on the road, my police problems had taken a back seat, although they were never out of my thoughts. Then one morning I had an apologetic letter from the solicitors. They had received a reply from my deputy chief constable dated the end of June, a copy of which they only now sent to me. I read the letter from the DCC with anger and growing disbelief; he was completely ignoring, effectively denying, that there had been any problems concerning my sexuality:

"Re: Special Constable Stephen Paul Johnson.

"I am in receipt of your letter dated the 23rd June 1993, concerning the above-named special constable.

"The meeting which took place on the 19th April 1993, between your client, Sub-Divisional Officer Rawles and divisional Commandant Haywood arose from concern for Mr Johnson. It had been necessary for Police Officers to visit his home a few days earlier following an emergency call indicating that your client was extremely depressed.

"I am advised that Mr Johnson mutually agreed with the Special Officers that he should temporarily refrain from performing Special Constabulary duties.

"Mr Johnson has since received the assistance of the Force Welfare Officer and other professional counselling. It would seem that he is making a satisfactory recovery.

"Special Constable Johnson's position is under review. As soon as I have satisfied myself that he is fully fit and able to safely resume duties, I shall be happy for him to continue with the Force.

"My officers will contact Mr Johnson in due course."

The bastards were lying through their teeth! What is more, that letter was dated 29 June, 1993, it was now 17 July and I had heard nothing. How much longer would they drag this all out? Were they still waiting for me to give in and resign? I spoke to my solicitor again and told him that I had heard nothing. He agreed to write to the deputy chief constable again. In the meantime, I was still waiting.

I turned my attention back to South Staffs Friends. I phoned the local offices of The Mercury, one of our local free papers. I spoke to Tim, their senior journalist and he agreed to meet me for a chat. We met, as arranged a few days later at their offices in the town centre. We walked over to a town centre pub and found a quiet corner where we discussed the new group over a pint. Tim was very enthusiastic and agreed to publicise South Staffs friends for us in the Mercury. I was careful only to use my first name and gave him the number for the CAB as a point of contact, as the CAB had kindly agreed to pass on any messages.

Rob Williams, the force welfare officer, phoned one morning and arranged to visit me again later the same morning. We had a pleasant chat, but what he had to tell me only reinforced what I already knew. Having achieved nothing when he had interrogated me, Superintendent Layton had later approached Rob Williams and asked him if he knew any details about my gay friends. Rob refused to tell him saying, as I had, that he had no right to that information.

After Rob had left, I phoned my solicitor again and told him this latest news. How much longer could they go on denying that they were homophobic and that this was the real reason I could not return to duty? No one who was gay was safe from the police within Staffordshire, I now realised. How many years had it taken me to realise this? The meeting I'd had with Simon in Stoke all those years ago came to mind when I'd fled from them after they were warning me not to trust Staffordshire Police!

The following Saturday I travelled down to London for the day with Andy. We were going to a BBC Prom concert at the Royal Albert Hall, but the trip also allowed me to meet Iain Ferguson at last and to thank him for the invaluable help he had given so far in trying to sort out my problems with Staffordshire Police. I met Iain outside the tube station at Sloane Square, and we set off for a restaurant he knew for a drink and a chat. He seemed pleased to see me, we had spent such a long time talking over the phone over the past two months and it was good to meet at last. Before parting, Iain promised to pass on my phone number to the LAGPA Midlands co-ordinator who was a West Midlands police officer living in Birmingham. Over the following few weeks, we made contact and met. I started to turn up for LAGPA social meetings at gay pubs in Birmingham and on one occasion, whilst in Gavan's, I ended up chatting and 'talking shop' with five other serving gay police officers. It made me realise that if on *one* night, in *one* gay venue, I could end up talking to *five* other gay police officers who knew *one* or more of the groups of us talking, how many other gay police officers were in Gavan's that night? How many were at other gay venues that night? How many were not out at a gay venue at all that night? How many gay police officers visit gay venues anyway? How many gay police officers were there? It was a revelation when I thought about it. But how many of them had made the mistake of telling their colleagues as I had? I became more determined than ever to fight and win, for theirs as much as for my own sake.

I turned my attention back to South Staffs Friends. After my success contacting The Mercury, I spoke to a journalist from The Post, the rival free newspaper in the area. Then I contacted the Stafford offices of The Post and persuaded them to give us publicity. In between times, I travelled over to see Paul and Gary in Wolverhampton on several occasions, and we set about designing the logo and promotional leaflets.

Small articles mentioning South Staffs Friends began to appear in the local papers. Straight away messages were left at the CAB. I began calling in every day to collect any left since the day before. I phoned up everyone who contacted us and arranged to visit them. News of the group spread rapidly, and other papers contacted the CAB and left messages for me to contact them. They were recognising that setting up such a group in a town like Rugeley merited at least a few column inches! I was becoming so wrapped up and busy organising South Staffs Friends that I was ignoring the fact that it had been almost two weeks since I had spoken to my solicitor and there was still no news. I phoned him one morning, but he had still not heard anything, which was frustrating.

Unexpectedly, later the same day, my solicitor phoned me back. Superintendent Layton had just phoned him to say that I could start back on duty; my SDO would inform me officially in a week or so! I'd won! They had given in! They had not succeeded in getting rid of their gay officer. I could not wait to tell all my friends!

Mixed with the general jubilation my friends warned me that it might not be the end. I thought about it, and I had to agree that after such a blatant and prolonged attack on me, Staffordshire Police had capitulated so very suddenly and without warning. Someone recommended that I watch my back, and I became worried once again.

After a day spent over at Paul and Gary's three days later designing our logo, I returned home to a message that Rob Rawles, my SDO had phoned. He would call me again the following morning. As arranged, the following morning Rob Rawles called me. He was noticeably short and to the point, it was obvious that he was making the call against his will.

"Steven, I have been instructed to let you know that you can start back on duty, but not for two or three days yet as I must go to a meeting first. I will let you know in a few days."

That was it. That was the result of all the shit they had put me through. No apology. No recognition they had done wrong. Just a short, terse message from Rob, obviously made against his will. But out of all that trouble, and because of it, a new gay support and social group was appearing. I waited for Rob's next call and returned to my work setting up South Staffs Friends, now in an extremely positive mood, buoyed up by the capitulation of Staffordshire Police.

My life had suddenly become very full, and I was working most of my waking hours setting things up, speaking to people over the phone and meeting them. I began filling an indexed book with contacts for any useful organisations, checking them all as I went along. As July had slipped into August our small group had already more than doubled in size. I drove over to Stafford one evening and met Haz and Joy, a 'straight' couple with a baby. Yet they were both bisexual and Haz was not the father of the baby; he had fled, leaving Haz and Joy to bring up his child. Both Haz and Joy were trained switchboard advisors, they worked on the Stoke switchboard, the same one I had contacted and fled from all those years earlier, soon after I had joined the police. They were both very keen that we were organising something for the South of the county and we were very keen to recruit them!

Dave and Tim also lived in Stafford, I called in to see them on the same evening I visited Haz and Joy. Tim, it turned out, was also a special constable, stationed in Stafford. He was not 'out' at his station, and I could not blame him.

We began to arrange weekly steering meetings on Monday evenings in the CAB offices. Very soon Sarah joined us, she lived in a village just outside Rugeley with her partner Thelma. Gary from Stafford contacted us, he had worked for Body Positive and would be especially useful. Cathy told me one day that she knew someone who wanted to join our group too, he was the new manager of a CAB office a few miles away across Cannock Chase, so Jeff joined our growing ranks. Now that our small group was approaching fifteen in number, meeting in the CAB offices was extremely useful. At least that would also get us used to working from there when the switchboard opened in a few weeks. Haz and Joy organised some basic training in telephone advice skills, utilising the training notes from Stoke.

I was delighted and surprised when Cathy called me; she had persuaded the manager of the pub which she had mentioned to me previously, that we might be able to hold our meetings in the lounge there on Wednesday evenings, to coincide with the switchboard night. I set off for the pub later that afternoon, eager to see the licensee and took Andy with me.

The pub was right on the main road through Rugeley, quite easy to find at the end of Horsefair. I had only ever visited it before when I had been on duty with the sergeant on licensed premises checks. We were greeted warmly and shown the room we could use. It was ideal; quite small and cosy, but it would easily hold thirty or forty people. I left shortly after, delighted that everything was moving forward so well and eager to tell the others.

We were still on target to open on 1 September, so I began contacting all the local papers again. Now that we had a reasonable number of volunteers, and still growing steadily, we needed to advertise the services of the new group.

Then, one Monday evening in mid-August I had a short, terse call from my SDO informing me that I could resume duties at any time. It had been so long since I had last been to the station that I did not know which shift would be on duty. I sat down and worked out the shift rotas since the spring, all those months earlier when I had last been on duty. Shift two was on nights, so they would be back working afternoons the following Thursday. I phoned the station and asked them to book me down for duty on the afternoon of August 26. At last, I could put it all behind me. I just hoped there would be no more dirty tricks.

In the meantime, I continued working with the new group. We were virtually all set up now and I was excited and waiting with eager anticipation for it all to go live. I had no idea how successful or otherwise it would be.

I finished off by contacting the newspapers in the region. They all agreed to give us some further publicity to say how successful we had been in getting volunteers and that the helpline and switchboard would be running every Wednesday from 1 September from seven thirty until nine p.m., together with the telephone number of the line we had been given to use.

As the end of August drew nearer, I became increasingly excited. Still, people were contacting us, offering their services. We set about organising a rota system for the switchboard. Cathy gave me a set of keys for the building, and the only thing we needed now was some good publicity in the regional papers the following week.

One morning near the end of August I drove my parents to the airport, they were going back to Switzerland for a fortnight. In normal circumstances, I would have been jealous, but I was becoming so excited and wrapped up in the final preparations for the launch of South Staffs Friends. Besides, Helen, my sister was going to the caravan for a week the following Friday and I would go away for the week with them. It would mean I would miss the first switchboard, but I needed a break desperately. The effect of the stress and pressure of the past few months was beginning to show, and over the past few weeks I had been working every hour I was awake.

Meanwhile, it was much more peaceful and relaxed at home as there were only my grandmother and me in the house. I just had to be a bit more careful when phoning people so that my nan did not overhear. Even though my parents both now knew and accepted that I was gay, we had decided not to tell my nan; at her age, we thought she would find it difficult to accept or understand.

We all turned up for our final Monday meeting at the CAB offices on 23 August. I was in a positive and happy mood; everything was reaching a climax at the same time. On Thursday I was resuming duties, on Friday I was going on holiday to the caravan finally and next week South Staffs Friends was going live.

I unlocked the back door and we all filed in, I was, as ever, eager to see if anyone else had contacted the CAB with offers of support. There was a note in Cathy's handwriting. Lisa, a journalist with the Staffordshire Newsletter wanted to speak to me about South Staffs Friends, she had seen it mentioned in other local papers. I had not even considered the Staffordshire Newsletter as a source for publicity, but any last-minute publicity would be very welcome. Everyone, including me, was in an exceptionally good mood and we had a productive meeting.

The following morning, I phoned the paper and asked to speak to Lisa. I was transferred a few seconds later.

"Hello, is that Lisa?"

"Yes, it is, how can I help you?"

"My name's Steve, from South Staffs Friends, I had a note that you phoned Rugeley CAB and wanted to speak to me."

"Oh yes! Steve! Thanks for getting back to me so quickly!"

"My pleasure, I suppose you have heard about our new group, I'm sorry that I did not contact the Newsletter sooner. Anyway, it would be great if you could give our group some publicity, the helpline opens for the first time next Wednesday evening, 1 September."

"Yes Steve, that's not a problem. Can I ask you a few

questions?"

"Yes, certainly, go ahead."

"Was it your idea to set up this group?"

"Well, sort of. It was the manager of the local CAB who suggested it in the first place, and then I set about organising it all with a few friends; it's been busy over the past few weeks!"

"Yes, I suppose it has! Anyway, Steve, can you tell me a bit about yourself?"

"What sort of thing do you want to know?"

"I understand that you are a special constable, is that right?"

How the hell did she know that? I panicked, not knowing what to say and it was several seconds before I answered her.

"Well, yes, but how do you know that?"

She continued, ignoring my question to her.

"Is it true that you set the group up after you were suspended from the specials because you are gay, and you had a lot of harassment from colleagues at the station?"

Suddenly this whole conversation had taken a quite different turn, and I didn't know what to say. How the hell did she know all of this? I did not know whether to admit it was the truth or deny it, but whatever I said, she already knew anyway. There was no way she could publish anything like that!

"Look, Lisa, I don't know what you've been told or where you got your information from, but any problems I might have had are over now. I am going back on duty on Thursday, I do not want this mentioned at all. Besides, I understood you wanted to speak to me to give some publicity to our new helpline."

"Is it true though, Steven?"

"I'm not prepared to talk about anything to do with the police, it's not relevant. I only wanted publicity for the helpline and that's the only thing I'm prepared to talk about."

"Have you got a telephone number I can call you back on?"

"No. If you want to contact me, do it through the CAB."

"OK, Steve. Anyway, the new helpline starts next Wednesday the 1st of September?"

"Yes, that's right. From seven thirty till nine, the number is the same as the one you called at the CAB."

"Right. OK then, Steve, I will be in touch. I hope it all goes well next week."

"OK, Lisa. But please do not mention my police background, it is not relevant, and I absolutely do not want it linked to the new group. Goodbye."

I put the receiver down, glad the call was over.

How the hell had she found out about that? My mind was working overtime running through every conceivable way it might have leaked out, but there was nothing. I had been incredibly careful not to tell anyone in the press. Except for Ian, the editor of Special Beat magazine down in London, when I had been trying to get a contact for Bill Piercy of NASCO. But it was not credible that Ian, down in London, would phone a local paper up here, coincidentally the one paper I had not yet spoken to, and besides he was a special himself and would not compromise my position like that. No, it was not him. My mind was desperately trying to work out who would have leaked that information, but nothing made sense! Anyway, I had made it quite clear to Lisa that I did not want it mentioned, and I hoped that would be the end of it.

But it was not. Later the same day Ian from Special Beat magazine phoned me up, he seemed concerned.

"Steven, I thought I'd better warn you. I had a journalist phone me earlier, from one of your local papers…"

My heart sank.

"Lisa, by any chance, from the Staffordshire Newsletter?"

"Yes, that's her. She was asking questions about your problems with your force. I didn't tell her anything, but she's on to something."

"Bloody Hell! How on earth has she got this information? No one I know has told her anything!" My heart sank.

"I understand Steve, I'm sure you wouldn't have told anyone from the press – it's a bit suspicious if you ask me..."

"Yes, I'm due to go back on duty in a couple of days, Staffordshire Police have just capitulated..."

"I really hope you can get to the bottom of it, Steve..."

"Thank you for letting me know Ian, I'm very grateful."

That conversation shocked me. How did she get on to Ian at Special Beat? Who told her about him, and how did she find out? I was becoming extremely worried – something was going on and I had a nasty, growing feeling it was another way in which Staffordshire Police were going to try to get rid of me. I phoned my friends, and we all agreed that no one from the new group had spoken to her, and it certainly was not anyone from the CAB because I checked. The best thing was to keep quiet, not to say anything. I had not given her any information; the only information she had was that which somehow, she had already got hold of herself. Hopefully, she would give up. I was rapidly regretting I had ever spoken to her.

Meanwhile, I had other matters to worry about. I pulled my uniform out of the wardrobe; it needed pressing and brushing. It had gathered dust over the past few months. I was slightly worried about going back to the station, unsure of the reaction I would get. But at last, it was only a day away now.

Late on Wednesday afternoon, a police patrol car pulled up outside. What did they want? An officer I did not know walked down the driveway; I went to the door.

"Is it Steve?"

"Yes?"

"The inspector wants to see you at the station. Can you pop down to see him at five?"

I thought for a few seconds. Why on earth did he want to see me? A chat about my returning to duty tomorrow?

"Yes, OK, I'll be there."

"Right, I'll let him know, bye."

And he was gone. Short and to the point. Suddenly I was worried. Was this another trick? After my last experience at headquarters, and knowing what Inspector Robertson thought of me, I wanted a witness with me, but despite asking, there was no one free I could arrange to go with me at such short notice.

An hour later I walked through into the foyer of the station. The security code had been changed on the door and I could not get in. I rang the bell and a few seconds later Sergeant Jones came to the hatch.

"The inspector has asked me to come down to see him, Sarge, can you let me in?"

"You can wait out there till he comes for you."

It was not a question. I was told to wait in the public foyer, they were not going to let me in. I felt humiliated and embarrassed.

I slumped down on the bench opposite, worried now about the purpose of this meeting, alarm bells were ringing again. It would be better if I walked out now and refused the meeting until I had a witness. But I sat and waited.

A patrol car pulled up outside. Four police officers walked up the steps and through the foyer past me and waited to be let into the station, completely blanking me out. It was extremely embarrassing. One hung back and I realised it was Richard. He was a probationary young PC now, but I knew him when he was a cadet at Rugeley only a year or two earlier.

"Hi, Steve! It's nice to see you again!" He smiled and held out his hand and we shook hands, in front of the other officers.

"I'm sorry about all the trouble you're having, I hope you get it sorted out soon. Good luck! Why are you waiting here?"

"The inspector wants to see me; they told me to wait out here. It's embarrassing."

"*I'm so sorry Steve!* The way you are being treated is disgusting! I really hope you get things sorted out soon!" He looked at me for several seconds as though he was about to say more, but then turned and with that, he disappeared through the door into the station with the other officers. It banged shut, locking me out.

Richard cheered me up. A lot. That was a genuine show of support and expressed so openly in front of other very senior officers who wouldn't even acknowledge me, and the sergeant who'd refused me entry. Richard was still a probationer, he still had to get through that yet; he was extremely brave.

I waited. An awfully long five minutes later the door opened. Inspector Robertson stood holding the door open for me, I felt slightly sick. He glared at me.

"Mr Johnson, follow me."

I said nothing, our mutual contempt for each other was plain for anyone to see. The door banged shut behind me, suddenly I was trapped in the station and that slightly sickening panic I'd recently experienced started to set in again.

I followed the inspector upstairs to an office.

"Mr Johnson to see you, sir," said the inspector, stepping back out of the office and shutting the door. I was left staring, shaking and frightened, at Superintendent Layton once again. I had been conned into coming down to the station. If I had known it was going to be Layton again, I would have refused absolutely. They knew it.

Layton looked at me for what seemed like ages; I couldn't work out what this was all about, but I sensed it wasn't good, and it was unnerving.

"Please take a seat, Mr Johnson," he said eventually, quite briskly.

I sat down.

For a short time, we sat in silence. I was silently screaming for help; I needed my friends urgently. I had to stay calm.

"Mr Johnson, I understand you have been speaking to the press rather a lot lately."

Suddenly I knew what it was all about. I thought for several seconds before replying, besides, it gave me time to compose myself. My mind was racing.

"I have spoken to a few local papers about a new group and helpline I have been involved in setting up. That's all, sir."

"Is it?"

"Yes sir, it is!" I replied emphatically.

"Well, Mr Johnson, a journalist from a local newspaper has contacted our press office at headquarters about you. You do realise, I am sure, that it is a serious disciplinary offence to speak to the press about internal matters without an authorisation?" he said as if he was enjoying twisting the knife in.

"I suppose you mean Lisa from the Staffordshire Newsletter?"

"So, you *have* been speaking to her then?"

"No! *she* contacted *me!*" I replied, emphatically, eager to explain what had happened, "She left a message with the CAB

206

for me to call her, which I did. I thought she wanted to publicise our new helpline, but when I spoke to her, she *already knew* about the problems I have been having here. I told her I did not want to speak about that, I said it wasn't relevant; I was starting back on duty, and I did not want it mentioned! All I wanted to speak about was the new helpline. I don't know how she found out about it all, but it was not from me or any of my friends!"

"You've spoken to quite a few papers recently, Mr Johnson."

"Yes, I know! What is wrong with that? It has got nothing to do with Staffordshire Police! I have spoken to several local papers to get publicity for our new support group. I never told any of them about my problems here! I only used my first name, and I used the CAB as a means of contact, go and ask them if you don't believe me!"

"Are you sure?"

"Of course, I am! Do you honestly believe that I would want my problems here, or just simply the fact that I am a serving police officer, linking to the new service? It would not exactly encourage people to ring up, would it?" I replied. The obvious point I was making did not seem to sink in. There was no reply from the superintendent, so I continued.

"I would also very much like to know *who* told Lisa about my problems here!" I continued, glaring at the superintendent, accusingly. Suddenly I remembered those warnings my friends had made about dirty tricks. I had fallen right into this one. Layton looked at the inspector sitting next to him for inspiration, he was getting nowhere once again.

"This journalist who phoned us said that you had claimed that you had been harassed by colleagues here at Rugeley because of your homosexuality."

"I have already told you, I never said anything to her about it!" I said more forcefully. I just restrained myself from saying *but it is the truth, though.*

"Mr Johnson, we are concerned about the allegations you have made. I would like to ask you now whether you want to make a formal complaint of harassment."

I panicked. I wasn't expecting that. This was too much like another trick; there just had to be a trick in it. What would happen if I made a formal complaint? They would suspend me again while it was investigated, and I had no confidence that it would be investigated properly. My mind was racing.

"I, I, er, I don't know; I'll have to think about it," I replied, eventually.

"Mr Johnson, I am giving you the opportunity now to make a formal complaint about the way you claim to have been treated. Do you want to or not?"

The more he pushed, the more certain I was that there was a trick in it somewhere.

"As I said, I'll have to think about it. I want to speak to my solicitor about it first."

"So, you do not want to make a formal complaint?"

"No, that is not what I said. I said I want to speak to my solicitor about it first, and I might make a complaint after speaking to my solicitor."

Once again, he was getting nowhere.

"Can you tell me about this new group you are involved in setting up?"

So, this was his next line of attack. I knew that as a police officer, I was not allowed to be involved with any political campaigning organisations, but South Staffs Friends was definitely not that.

"What do you want to know?" I replied, wearily. I was

rapidly losing my patience with all their tricks; they were not giving in easily.

"What exactly is the group?"

"It is a support helpline, somewhere for gay people in mid-Staffordshire to phone if they need advice, help or support. If they have problems at work, for instance…" I said very pointedly – I waited to see if the point I was making had sunk in but if it had, the superintendent didn't show it. "It also helps the families and friends of gay, lesbian, or bisexual people. We are also organising a social group alongside it. That is *all* it is. We are working through the Citizens Advice Bureau, and we have support from the local health authority. It is not a political organisation."

"Who else is involved with this group?"

Here we were again! Once more Staffordshire Police were digging for any information they could get about my friends.

"Just a few friends, that's all. Plus, several people have volunteered to help because of the publicity.

"Can you tell me who these friends are?"

"No, I cannot, that is none of your business."

"Does it include Paul and his friend Gary?"

"Of course."

"Are Paul and Gary still together as partners?"

"I'm not answering that."

My temper was not far from boiling over, but this was developing into a game of wills and I had to stay calm and in control.

"Does the chief constable know about this new helpline?"

My temper flared.

"Staffordshire Police have stuck their nose into my private life far too much lately, *it's none of your bloody business!*" I shouted, my temper boiling over.

"But it is our business." Layton replied very calmly, "You should have informed the chief constable what you were doing when you were setting up this group."

"What I do in my private life is *my* business! I'm becoming sick of the way you are interfering in it!"

"Nevertheless, Mr Johnson, I suggest that if you want to continue serving you should write and let the chief constable know what the new helpline is about."

I glared at him. There was another uneasy silence.

"And you are sure that you do not want to make a formal complaint of harassment?"

"As I said earlier, not before speaking to my solicitor. I am not trying to create any problems, I never have. If you sort out the problems which I have had with some of the officers here properly so that I can get back on duty, then I will be satisfied, that's all I want!"

There was another uneasy silence for several seconds.

"Well, that will be all for now. Until you hear further you must not go on duty."

That stopped me dead. The bastards! I *knew*, I *absolutely* knew they would find a way to get at me again, and this was it!

"But I was supposed to be starting back again tomorrow sir!" I replied, with an air of exasperation.

"Not now, not until we have investigated further. In the meantime, I suggest you write to the chief constable. And do not say any more to the press. That will be all."

I got up and walked quickly out of the office, ran down the back stairs and out of the back door.

The fucking bastards! So that had been the trick I had been warned that might happen! It was *them* who had spoken to the press, conveniently leaking the issue I was having, to discredit me and give the chief constable a reason to dismiss me, the very week I was to resume duties. It was all so bloody obvious now. But it had not worked for them, thankfully!

I was once again suspended though. It hit me like a brick wall. I had built myself up to return to the station, and now I was back at square one. Not for the first time I had serious doubts about whether I would ever sort this mess out, not while this chief constable was in charge.

I spent Thursday, the day I should have been back on duty, getting advice from anyone I could. Working out, trying to guess what their next trick would be, trying to stay one step ahead of them. I phoned my solicitor again and told him what had happened. I spoke to Iain Ferguson again. We all concluded that trying to get me to make a formal complaint certainly *was* a trick. I was advised to keep my nerve; with any luck continuing pressure would force them to capitulate. Again. But if it did not happen soon, I knew I couldn't keep this up. My anxiety was growing again, and it was slowly grinding me down.

I went to bed early that night, I was exhausted. On top of everything else, I had to hide this from my nan. How could she understand the complexities of what I was going through? Anyway, I had planned going to Wales with Helen and Neil tomorrow afternoon. A break at the caravan would be very welcome now. I left the packing for the morning; I was too exhausted.

Early the next morning I was woken from my sleep by the phone ringing. I looked at the clock, it was seven thirty-five a.m. Who would ring at this time in the morning? There was only my nan and me in the house. I dragged myself reluctantly out of bed and reached for the phone. "Hello?"

"Hello, is that Steve?" It was Sarah from the social group.

"Yes, how can I help Sarah?" Why was she ringing me this early in the morning?

"Steve, I thought I ought to phone you, sorry it's so early. On my way to work, I picked up a copy of the Staffordshire Newsletter, just now, and you ought to know…" She hesitated before continuing "…they have put you on the front page, you are the main story…"

I stood, fiddling with the phone cable, unsure what to say or take in what she had said. I was numb. I didn't know what to say, I was mute.

"…Steve, are you still there? Are you OK?"

"Yes, yes. What does it say?" I asked eventually.

"Well…you're not going to like this. The headline reads: "'*Special cop opens gay line, policeman claims harassment*'. The text reads as follows; '*A gay Rugeley special constable is launching a lesbian and homosexual helpline in South Staffordshire next week. Steve Johnson claims he decided to start the line after he was harassed by workmates at Rugeley Police Station because of his sexuality… He said I had a lot of problems when I decided to come out a few months ago…They tried everything to get rid of me…I was questioned about my sexuality, about who my boyfriend was and about what I got up to and what we did together. I can go back on duty this week, but I am expecting a lot of problems…The thirty-four-year-old special constable of Bracken Way Rugeley is currently unemployed but has worked for Staffordshire Police as a part-time officer for six years. Staffordshire Police have denied Mr Johnson's allegations of harassment. Deputy Chief Constable Gordon said we have received no complaints and I have no evidence at all that this person has been victimised in any way by*'…just a minute while I turn the paper over, it continues on the back…" The sound of rustling paper… "Here we are, it goes on; *'Staffordshire Police. Since his revelation he has been offered every proper consideration. His current position as a member of the special constabulary is being given consideration in the light of the most recent events. The aim of the new helpline called South Staffordshire Friends is not just to provide advice for gay people according to Mr Johnson. It is also to provide a support group for the gay community outside Stoke-on-Trent and Birmingham. He said it will be a chance for people to meet and talk about their problems. The helpline goes live on Wednesday night and so far, the group running from the Citizens Advice Bureau, Anson Street, Rugeley, has around thirty members.'*… Steve. I am deeply sorry. I just thought I ought to warn you before the press inevitably starts phoning. They're bastards! Are you OK?"

I was very definitely not OK. I couldn't think clearly now.

"Yes, thanks for letting me know, Sarah," I said quite weakly.

"I've got to go now, Steven. I am on my way to work. I'll give you a call a bit later, you've got my work number if you need it?"

"Yes."

"Good. Phone me if you need me. Good luck. I will try to get over to see you later. Don't let the bastards get to you. I'm sorry to have to give such bad news, but I had to let you know."

"Yes, I understand. Thank you, Sarah. I'll speak to you later."

I replaced the handset. My mind was racing.

Everything was getting out of hand, seriously out of hand now. I was on my own in the house with my nan. I had been 'outed' in a spectacular way! If I had been dealing with coming

213

out slowly and carefully for the past year or so, that was all history now. Everyone would know! Absolutely everyone. How could I keep it from my nan now? I kept going over and over the same thing, so many thoughts in my mind were tumbling out of control, and I was panicking. Anyone and very probably everyone in Rugeley, or even Staffordshire, *anyone* would know I was gay now. And where I lived. The neighbours! All the troublemakers, the lawbreakers whom I regularly dealt with. Anyone. What was going to happen?

I looked nervously out of the window; the street was quiet. Normal. My life had been turned upside down and inside out all at once. My nan was in the next bedroom in bed still fast asleep. I knew the phone would start ringing again very soon. Quickly and quietly, I got dressed. I didn't want to disturb the peace and calm of the house, which was in complete contrast to the utter turmoil going on inside me. I didn't want Nan to wake up into the nightmare that was about to erupt.

I tiptoed downstairs and walked through into my room at the back, picked up the telephone there, set it on the floor near the fire and sat down next to it, confidently expecting it to start ringing at any time. I urgently needed to speak to someone, I needed help. I was shaking uncontrollably. It was still early, too early to phone anyone. But I needed help, I was frightened. What was going to happen now? I was on my own in the house with my nan, I kept reminding myself. My whole family – my parents and my sister Caroline, and Chris were all on holiday. I was supposed to be going away later, but how could I go now, leaving my nan to cope with everything?

I sat and stared at the phone. Suddenly, as soon as I looked down at it, it started ringing and it was still early. It made me jump; my nerves were on edge. I nervously picked up the receiver.

"Hello?"

"Can I speak to Mr Steve Johnson, please?"

"That's me, who is it?"

"I'm a journalist from the Sun newspaper. Can I speak to you about your problems with your police force?"

"I'm sorry, I'm not allowed to. No comment."

"Can you tell me what happened at your station, I see that you claim you were harassed by colleagues because you told them you are gay, is that true?"

"No Comment!" I slammed the receiver down.

Shit! It was starting. I could hear movement upstairs; the noise of the phone ringing had woken my nan and she was getting up. The phone rang again; it was the Express and Star, one of the regional papers. Again, 'no comment' and I replaced the receiver.

My nerves were frayed, and I couldn't stand much more. I noticed I was starting to feel nauseous. I tried to do some simple mental arithmetic, but I couldn't, my brain had shorted and frozen. I walked back through into the lounge and looked once again out of the window. The street was coming to life, it was almost nine. My nan was coming downstairs, so I walked quickly back into my room at the back, I could not cope with her, I could not hide my fraught state.

I picked up the phone and dialled Helen, my sister. I told her what had happened and explained that I would not be able to go with them to the caravan now. She was concerned and said she would be down very shortly. I called Paul and he was equally as worried. He told me to keep in touch and let me know of any developments.

The phone rang again, my nerves were on edge, and I didn't want to answer it. But it was Cynthia, my mother's sister phoning to say she would be over as planned with her Son Neil a bit later. I had forgotten she was coming – she was coming to stay with nan while I went away with my sister. I told her what had happened and explained everything as briefly as I could.

The rest of the morning was a blur, I remained rooted to the floor sitting by the phone. My pulse rate soared every time it rang, and it rang a lot. Mostly concerned friends, but the occasional journalist too. I was waiting for the abusive calls. How could I hide this from my nan now? Everyone and anyone would know I was gay. I was glad when Helen turned up and soon after Cynthia arrived with Neil, too. Other friends arrived but I was in such a state that it was all a nightmarish blur.

I pulled Helen to one side and told her there was no way I could go away for a whole week with them and leave Nan, how would she cope when she found out, as she surely must? Helen sat me down and calmed me down.

"Steven, Nan knows about you. I have just been talking to Cynthia. Nan told Cynthia she found out about you yesterday."

"But how?" I asked, incredulously.

"You won't like this, but Nan answered a phone call while you were out. Someone on the other end, we don't know who, but it was male, and they asked for you. Nan told him you were out, but that she was your grandmother and could take a message. He then told her that her fucking grandson was a fucking queer puff or words to that effect. Anyway, it was not very pleasant."

I stared at Helen.

"I'm sorry Steve. But at least she knows now."

"She didn't say anything!"

"I know, but that's what nan's like isn't it?"

"She never gave anything away either, she hid it very well."

Then it struck me. Nan had taken that call *yesterday*. At that

216

time, my sexuality was not common knowledge, as it is today; the Newsletter was not published until this morning. Yesterday, the only people who knew about me were my closest friends from the caving group whom I had not seen for years, and it was too much of a coincidence to be them calling right now, besides, they wouldn't do that. Then there were my gay friends, but it was certainly not them. Neither would it be the staff from the CAB. It only left one source. And yesterday was the day I had been due to start back at the station. And with growing realisation and horror, the call was conveniently timed for when I was *out* for my meeting at the station. It was *them*. It was a Staffordshire Police officer. It could only be them.

I got up suddenly and ran upstairs to my bedroom, I couldn't cope with everyone around me. I sat down on the bed. I felt extremely sick now. I was angry and I was very frightened. How low would they stoop now? What else might they do? At what level would they stop? I was panicking.

I pulled the phone towards me and called Paul.

"Paul, it's me."

"Steven, what's happened, I was about to call you, we're both very concerned."

"Paul, I've been getting calls from the press all morning, I was worried about my nan…"

"I know Steven, I understand."

My eyes were hot and wet, and I could not control myself any longer.

"Paul, she knows! The bastards phoned her anonymously yesterday and told her about me in an abusive phone call. Paul, *please help!*" I was crying uncontrollably; the tears were streaming down my face.

"Steven, stay there, keep calm, it's all right. We're coming straight over, try not to worry."

I replaced the receiver and lay back on the bed, the room was spinning around; I felt sick. I lost track of how long I lay there staring at the ceiling.

Eventually, the sickness subsided. I pulled myself together and wandered back downstairs. Sarah had turned up; they were all sitting in my room having some sort of conference. I wandered in and sat down.

"I had to come over to see you, Steven. We're all very worried about you," said Sarah.

"Thanks for coming, it's appreciated. But I'm worried about what's going to happen now."

Paul and Gary arrived; Paul looked concerned. He was talking to my aunt and my sister in the lounge. Eventually, he came through.

"Steven, we've had a bit of a conference. We are taking you away from here for a few days. You're coming back to stay with us in Wolverhampton. You need the break."

"But I can't!" I pleaded, "I cannot leave Nan on her own here. Mum and Dad are still on holiday. I can't leave her to cope with all of this!"

"Steven, it's all been arranged, it's OK. Your aunt and cousin are here, remember. We have sorted everything, try not to worry about that. Go and get your things ready."

I was not in a state to argue, I could not think enough for that.

"But..."

"Just go and get ready."

I got up and went upstairs and began packing my bag. This was all unreal. Paul came up the stairs. I walked out onto the landing with my bag. We stood and looked at each other; I was

218

shaking. Paul walked over put his arms around me and squeezed me tightly.

"It's OK now, Steven. Just forget about it all for a bit, we have taken care of everything. Are you ready?"

Chapter 11

Breakdown

That day was a low point. I had never felt so bad, so helpless, so angry, and so frightened all at the same time. And as Paul and Gary drove me back over to their house in Wolverhampton, I felt guilty that I was leaving my nan behind to sort out the mess which would not even exist if it were not for me.

Everything had been taken care of. Paul had explained the problem to Neil before we left; he would stay and look after my nan for a few days until I returned. Paul did not give him a contact number for us, that way Neil could genuinely say he did not know where I was when anyone phoned. And he would field every call to the house, and my nan would not have to answer any calls. We would phone regularly to check that they were all OK. Effectively, I was spirited away, cut off from the media, from the abusive phone calls and the police, completely.

It still did not make me feel any less guilty, I still felt responsible, despite being repeatedly told that I was not. But I was not able to argue, everything was a blur, I still could not think clearly, and I was still numb with shock. We walked around to the takeaway for a Chinese meal soon after arriving, it cheered me up slightly, but I was still in a world of my own, isolated.

As Paul left me to make my bed in the lounge later in the evening, he walked over and gave me a reassuring hug before leaving to join Gary upstairs. I sat in silence for a long time, staring at the fireplace. I was a fugitive. And I was 'outed' to everyone. What would be the consequence of my headline 'outing'? I didn't care now, it had happened, and there was nothing I could do about it.

As I made and climbed into my bed, a thought appeared from my troubled mind; this might have been all a good thing. Now I didn't have to worry about hiding my sexuality from anyone at all, I just didn't care any more.

My forced exile gave me time to work with Paul on finishing the leaflets. As the weekend progressed, the shock subsided. I phoned home several times and spoke to Neil but, to my relief and surprise, there had been virtually no more calls and no trouble. None of the neighbours had said anything.

I planned to return home on Wednesday evening when we would all go to the first switchboard session. As the weekend progressed and the shock and numbness decreased it was replaced with new confidence and optimism. I didn't care any more who knew that I was gay. We even managed to joke about my 'celebrity' status.

By Monday evening I was beginning to feel homesick, I was worried about leaving my nan for so long and I still felt guilty for leaving in the first place, although I had to admit to myself that I hadn't been of much use to anyone at the time. Early on Tuesday morning, Paul drove me home. As we approached Rugeley I began to feel sick, my stomach was tight, and I was nervous. The condition worsened as we drove onto the estate and down the street. I was very conscious of people watching me as I carried my bag into the house, but probably no one had even noticed. Paul left a few minutes later.

I was glad to be home, there had been no problems in my absence and very few calls. My nerves were still on edge, and I still jumped a mile when the phone rang a few minutes after returning. It was a reporter from a local radio station wanting an interview. It all seemed far too much of a coincidence that the first call, only a few minutes after I had returned home, four days after leaving, was the first call from the media since leaving, wanting to talk about my so-called revelation. Was I being paranoid? Luckily, after that, there were no more calls. Everything was ready for the launch of the helpline the following evening. I just hoped that now that I was linked to it people would not be put off from calling. There was no way of ever knowing.

The following evening, I drove down to the CAB excited and curious as to whether we would receive many calls. I met Haz and Joy in the car park and we let ourselves in. Gradually the others turned up, the clock was slowly ticking around towards seven-thirty. We sat waiting expectantly. On cue, at seven-thirty, the phone rang. Edward, who had recently joined the helpline volunteers, picked up the phone. It was a short but odd conversation, and I was curious to find out what it was about.

"What was that?" I asked as Edward replaced the phone.

"It was a gay, sorry, a homosexual man who objected to us using the word 'gay' in our publicity!"

The phone rang again.

Later we set off for the pub, our first social meeting. Haz helped me lock up and carry everything out to the car. We drove eagerly round to the pub to see how the first social was progressing. If it were half as successful as the first switchboard had been, I would be pleased.

We walked eagerly into the pub, and I was surprised to see that the room was busier than I had expected, everyone who had contacted us over the past few weeks was there. A dozen calls and fourteen people at our first social, was much better than I dared to hope for! It was an encouraging sign that the group would grow over the following few weeks. We had a new member of our group too, Steve from Stafford.

Over the following few months, we became good friends and Steve is now confident about his own sexuality. But as far as my other friend, Steve Smith was concerned, I was still getting nowhere. I tried once more to arrange to go out for a drink one evening. I phoned him to see when he might be free, but this time he was quite blunt. He made it plain that it was very awkward and that he did not want to see me socially. I put the phone down on him abruptly, I was shocked that such a loyal and trusted friend could turn against me so very much. I was completely cut off from the station and my former life now.

I had seen the conflict between the gay community and the police all those years earlier when I had phoned the Stoke switchboard soon after joining the specials. I had rejected that society then, it seemed alien. I could not understand their utter distrust and contempt for the police, but I had been naive. Now that it had been rammed home to me very forcefully just how much open hatred there is of gay people by the police service in Staffordshire, from lower-ranking officers right to the very top, and so openly and officially expressed, I could very easily understand the distrust shown by the gay community all those years earlier. Despite trying to remain neutral I was being pushed forcibly away by the police and I was turning increasingly to my gay friends and the gay community. Now I too distrusted the police utterly, yet I was still a serving officer, and I *did* want to go back. It was opening another conflict within me. Did I really want to go back?

On the advice of one or two friends from LAGPA, I eventually phoned and spoke to the force's Equal Opportunities

Officer, Inspector Drayton. I was very wary of any senior officers from headquarters by now and had been very reluctant to phone him earlier, not seriously believing he would help. Yet he seemed glad that I had contacted him and wanted to speak to me. I made an appointment and once again a few days later I set off for headquarters. The difference this time was that it was a meeting which I had arranged.

I still felt sick as I drove into the grounds of headquarters. I waited in the foyer, desperate to get away from the place again, it reminded me too much of my last visit. But I didn't have to wait long, Inspector Drayton came down for me straight away and led me to his office. I was introduced to a training sergeant who was also present. So far, so good.

Inspector Drayton asked me to outline everything which had happened. He explained that he had been aware of my situation but could not get involved until I asked to see him in case it compromised his professional position if I made an official complaint. I took a deep breath and began. I left nothing out, I told them the whole, dirty truth. I paused several times, unsure of how they would react to what I was saying, but by the time I had finished, both officers seemed genuinely shocked at the extent and level of the homophobia and the treatment I had received. I was assured that the matter would be investigated and dealt with urgently and that I really could trust them. I did – almost. I left the meeting thirty minutes later with my trust in Staffordshire Police slightly restored.

The success of South Staffs Friends' first night was repeated and built upon over successive weeks. The number of calls to the helpline fluctuated, sometimes ten to fifteen calls in an evening and sometimes only three or four, but we always had some calls. And the letters started to flood in. A lot were letters from people wanting help, some were abusive, and a few quoted the bible in attacking us, some of them were amusing. But there were also several letters supporting me from people who had seen the Staffordshire Newsletter, one even sent me a billboard advertising the Newsletter for the week I was featured. I would frame it!

I had worried that linking my police career to the group would put people off, but it did not seem to, although it was impossible to tell how many might have called otherwise. But in one respect it did generate a few calls from serving police officers, or people we presumed were, but would not say so outright through fear and distrust, which I could well understand. One police officer living a few miles away desperately wanted to talk; he used his partner as a point of contact, but although I tried to reassure him through his partner that he could trust us, he never did. He desperately needed to talk to someone. I felt helpless, but it showed, if nothing else, the wretched state in which gay police officers could find themselves.

For the sake of these officers, if not for me I realised, I had to get back on duty as soon as possible, to prove to other officers by example that being gay did not have to be a problem. Reluctantly, as asked, I wrote to the chief constable and told him officially of the existence of South Staffs Friends. I made it clear what the group was, but also what it was not. I wonder what sort of fuss they would have made had it been the caving group I used to run. None whatsoever. It angered me that just because this was a gay support group that they insisted on being told about it, it proved beyond any doubt that their prejudice against gay people was very real and still strongly and officially expressed, right to the top. I did not want to write the letter; Staffordshire Police had pried into my private life far too much over the past few months and the police service was not even my career! But I was rapidly losing patience. I posted the letter and waited for the next round of the battle.

South Staffs Friends social group very quickly became just as successful as the helpline. It grew in numbers steadily from the first week until by early October we were getting an average of thirty people every week, sometimes more. People of all ages, from teenagers to people in their sixties, both men and women, gay and bisexual and from a wide area. Several were local, but many others travelled from Stafford, Cannock, or Lichfield. One travelled down from Stoke every week, and another came up from Redditch. As the weeks progressed and everyone got to know each other, the atmosphere relaxed and I always eagerly looked forward to Wednesday evenings. Having been given sole responsibility for the CAB offices and the key for them, I spent the first half of the evening with two or three other volunteers at the CAB, arranged by rota every week, before moving on to the pub at nine.

South Staffs Friends could not have been more successful, much more successful than anyone had imagined, and it showed just how much of a need there had been for such a service in the area. People continually told us they were amazed that such a service and social group existed in Rugeley, of all places! Despite the effort needed to get it all going, I was amazed too!

By mid-October we had a new influx of people, they had travelled over from Lichfield and Walsall, and the word was spreading fast about the group. Trevor was one of the new members and he quickly showed his enthusiasm to help. I was pleased that someone was prepared to take some of the load off me, running between the switchboard and the pub was a juggling act sometimes. Trevor helped to sort out the social group, for which I was extremely grateful, and he quickly settled in by organising a Christmas party. The success of the service since it had started had been overwhelming, I was in an extremely positive mood and looking forward to 1994 which was not too far away.

But all was not quite right. The first I noticed was that Paul was coming down to the group less often; he was having relationship problems with Gary and needed some time away from the group. There were mutterings from some members of the social group that Haz and Joy were not welcome because they were bisexual and not gay. I found this attitude disgusting and fully supported them, but ultimately that support was used against me. It was too much to expect everything to be perfect, I thought. Something like this was only to be expected. By early November Paul and Gary seemed to have resolved their differences and to my relief were back together again, although I saw much less of them now than I had.

As the days and weeks passed, I became increasingly frustrated that I'd had no decision back from the chief constable. I phoned headquarters again and spoke to Rob Williams, the force welfare officer, to find out whether he had heard anything. He had. The force was going to send a chief inspector to take charge at Rugeley for a while, over Inspector Robertson. He hinted that she would be very much *on my side*. I spoke to Inspector Drayton again and he also thought I was going to be able to return to the station very soon, although he could not talk for long as H.M. Inspectors of Constabulary were descending on headquarters to scrutinise the personnel department at extremely short notice, and he had a lot of work to do to get it ready. That really pleased me. Why had the HMI's chosen to visit just the personnel department when the force had been officially visited by the HMI's only the year before for a full inspection? Most of my problems had originated from the personnel department, and I knew the Home Office had been aware of my problems. It didn't take much to connect the two. Staffordshire Police were being put under pressure at government level.

A few days later I received a message that Chief Inspector Wattwood wanted to see me at the station for a chat. The summons to see the chief inspector left me in a dilemma. I had learnt my lesson, I would not attend any more summons to see senior officers without a witness being present, even though Rob Williams had said Chief Inspector Wattwood was *on my side*. In the event, I could not find anybody suitable who could go with me as a witness at such short notice. As a substitute, Paul offered to lend me a small tape recorder which I could hide in my pocket, at least I would have a taped record of the meeting, even if, as I well knew, it was a disciplinary offence to do such a thing. But I was desperate and unapologetic.

At the appointed time I presented myself at the station once again, the tape recorder concealed in my jacket pocket. I realised that I now felt sick every time I approached the station. I was shown up to the same office I had been interrogated in last time, I managed to switch the tape recorder on without being noticed on the way up. I was introduced to Chief Inspector Wattwood and another inspector.

The meeting was much more relaxed than my earlier experiences. The chief inspector had an ultimatum to give me. The chief constable would let me back on duty provided I undertook to end my role working on the helpline. I protested that it was a backward step, I knew other police officers in other forces who were encouraged to work with advice and counselling services. But she was adamant that it was policy in this force that no officer could do so. I made it truly clear what I thought of that policy and reluctantly agreed that I would refrain from answering any calls – if they assured me that it applied to every officer in the force and for whatever type of helpline or counselling service, and I was assured that it was. But they could not stop me from helping to run South Staffs Friends. I was told that I could resume duties at any time.

It was extremely embarrassing and awkward when, a minute or two before the meeting ended, there was a high-pitched whistling which was coming from my pocket. Nothing was said and I left the meeting in a hurry. Paul had not told me that the machine whistled like that when the tape ran out!

Once again, there was no form of apology, no acceptance that the force had grossly mistreated me. Indeed, I had been made to feel like the one who had to grovel to get back, I was still seen as the culprit. It angered me. They had kept me off duty for seven months. I worked out when my shift would be on duty. Early the following Wednesday morning I changed into my uniform for the first time in several months and set off for the station. I felt physically sick when I approached it, and I hesitated before opening the back door. What reception would I receive?

The station was quiet. I spent the first hour or so in the control room, it felt odd. It was as if I was starting all over again. It was not easy making conversation. The chief inspector phoned down from her office and asked me to pop up and see her.

I knocked on her door and walked in.

"Hello Steven, come in and sit down."

"Thank you, Ma'am."

I pulled up a chair and sat down.

"Well, first of all, how are you finding it being back on duty?"

"OK. But I have only been here a short time yet, but it's good to be back again." I lied, concealing the fact that I was finding the whole experience, since entering the station, extremely unnerving.

"Anyway, Steven, there's something else I want to see you about."

I was puzzled and alarmed.

"Did you know that it is a disciplinary offence to tape-record meetings and interviews, other than the official taped interview of suspects of course, without the authority of the chief constable?"

Now I knew what she was getting at.

"No, sorry Ma'am, I did not." I lied.

"Well, I have to instruct you that it is." She paused for a few seconds. "And you were taping that meeting we had here last week, weren't you?"

I thought for a few seconds before answering. Her question had not come across as particularly threatening.

"Ma'am, all I want to say is that as a result of the way I have been treated by senior officers in the force over the past few months, and as I had not got time to arrange for a witness to come with me last week, I reserved the right to take any precautions I felt necessary to safeguard my interests. That's all I'm prepared to say, Ma'am."

I was pleased with my answer. Chief Inspector Wattwood smiled at me, she almost seemed pleased with it herself.

"OK Steven, you are now aware of the force policy about taping. Anyway, you can go back on duty. That is all."

"Thank you, Ma'am."

I got up and walked out of the office. I guessed she did not blame me at all for what I had done but couldn't say so officially.

I went back down to the control room.

I was glad when Kev called in to pick me up for a drive around, after that, I spent time walking around the town centre before returning to the station and booking off duty at two. I left the station as quickly as possible; I had felt extremely uncomfortable just being there.

It had been my first duty back, an important symbolic gesture but also a pointer to the way the situation was at the station now. I hated it. I felt extremely uncomfortable, nervous, and jumpy, unsure whether I was about to get stabbed in the back again. I didn't know who I could trust, or who if anyone, was on my side. Looked at like that, I trusted no one. It was becoming clear that the publicity in the paper accusing officers at the station of harassment had not exactly helped me, it had turned those officers who had supported me against me now. How would I ever be able to convince them that it wasn't me who'd said anything about it to the press? – although I believed that I would have been justified in doing so.

It was a 'catch-22' situation. I could not say anything to the press without facing severe disciplinary proceedings and then being dismissed, which I did not want. I wanted to remain a serving special, but at the same time I wanted to shout out to everyone who would listen, just what bastards Staffordshire Police had been, it would make me feel much better. But I couldn't say anything because that would not achieve anything other than short-term satisfaction for me, it would not help in the long term. For that, I had to remain silent and continue serving. They knew that and so did I. I felt terrible.

All the positive fighting spirit I'd had for the past few months had vanished. For so long I had been on a roller coaster which was out of control, which was both exhilarating and frightening. I'd had something to fight, something to push against but now it was all gone, I had nothing to fight. And I was still angry. There was still no acknowledgement of wrongdoing or even an apology on their behalf. I still felt like the wrong-doer, and I'd had to grovel to get back.

It started snowing during the afternoon, quite heavily. It did not stop and by teatime, it was quite thick and beginning to drift. I was worried that the switchboard volunteers would not be able to make it to Rugeley. I phoned Joy and Edward, they would try and make it, but they might be late. I had no choice but to go myself, open it up and hope they made it on time.

It only took me a couple of minutes to drive there normally, but it took ten; how long would it take those coming from Stafford? As seven-thirty approached and no one had shown up, I was quite worried. The helpline would be live in a minute, and I was not supposed to take any calls. But they would not know, would they?

Car headlights turned into the drive at the side of the building, and someone had arrived at last, to my relief. But then the phone rang, and I had no choice but to answer it.

"Hello, South Staffs Friends, can I help you?"

"Hello, is that Steven?" It was a male voice.

"No…Steven's not here yet, my name's Mark, can I help you?"

"Not really, I need to speak to Steven."

"Is it some information you need, or do you need to talk about something else? I can help you."

"No. It is all right. If I phone back later, can I speak to Steven, then?"

"Well not really, Steven doesn't answer the calls, so really it would have to be someone else, are you sure I can't help you, or pass a message on to Steven when he gets here?"

"No, it's OK, thanks."

The line went dead. I put the phone down as Haz and Joy walked in.

"Hi, Steve! Sorry, we're late, but we got here in the end."

It was a huge relief to see them!

"Thank heaven you got here! The bastards have only just been checking up on me, asking to speak to me by name, trying to catch me out! They weren't even very clever or subtle about it either!"

From now on I would have to be incredibly careful, we decided that under no circumstances would I answer any more calls.

The social meeting was busier than we had expected but was still quieter than usual. I returned home later that evening depressed and very unsettled. That call had only served to unsettle me further. How far and for how long were Staffordshire Police going to pry into my private life? The reality was that they were *still* trying to find something they could use against me. It was going to be extremely difficult if not impossible to get back to some normality where we trusted each other. Indeed, it seemed utterly impossible. My first duty back at the station had only shown just what an uphill struggle I had ahead of me to be accepted again. I was beginning to realise that I never would be accepted again in the way I had been.

Colleagues saw me as a radical extremist, and I now was. I never had been, I had fitted in quite happily and kept the status quo. But simply resisting their attempts to push me out had painted me into a corner as a radical and that was unacceptable in the police service, it did not fit comfortably with the canteen culture where all the 'lads' were fighting together, on the same side. So, how could I ever have won?

My anger was just as intense as it had ever been, but now I had nothing to push against, nothing to fight. There was no outlet for the anger, I became frustrated, and I was impotent.

No one in the group could see or understand what I was going through, they were oblivious to the fact that I was now being torn apart. All the bitter anger and frustration of the past few months was coming to the surface now that it was all over. But there was no outlet, nowhere to target it. It was growing inside me at an alarming rate, and I was becoming very frightened, I knew it had to come out somehow.

My parents had gone away for a few days, and once again I was alone with my nan. I could not tell her how I was feeling; she had been very understanding of my sexuality, and it had not been a problem, but I could hardly understand what was happening to me myself and I did not want to alarm her. I phoned some of my friends from the social group but could barely explain what was happening and I did not want to bother Paul, he was sorting things out with Gary, making a deliberate effort to distance himself from me and the rest of the group.

I shut myself in my bedroom, keeping out of my nan's way. I walked around the room, lay on the bed, and then got up and started walking around the room again feeling ever more trapped and frightened. I wanted to cry and scream but I couldn't. Inside I was screaming silently, but I must not frighten my nan.

For two days I kept myself locked in the bedroom as the pressure increased; I was going insane, and I knew it. Then I was angry that no one understood, no one *could* understand. My nan brought me a cup of tea. After she had left, I threw it against the opposite wall. I looked at myself in the mirror and hated what I saw, so I punched out at the mirror repeatedly, until it cracked and shattered, falling to pieces as shards of blood-stained glass fell to the floor, blood dripping from my hands onto the shards. At least now I couldn't see myself. I ripped my posters off the wall, tore them up and turned to my pen drawings of Switzerland which I had laboured over for hundreds of hours. I tore them to pieces. For hour after agonising hour, I slowly destroyed my bedroom. I picked up a red marker pen from the mess and chaos on the floor, I threw the top across the room and began scrawling on the by now free space on the walls *'Why does everybody stab me in the back? People are SHIT! Why did you never support me? I spend all my life helping people. What a prat!'* Then in even larger, wilder writing; *'BASTARDS.'* Then I turned to the opposite wall and wrote; *'FUCKING SHITS'* in huge, scrawling letters. I threw the pen on the floor.

I collapsed, exhausted onto the floor, amidst the torn posters, the torn shreds of my drawings and the shards of broken glass, the blood, and I cried. And cried. Finally, I found some peace as I drifted off into a dreamless sleep. It was dark when I woke up. The worst of the anger was gone.

It did the trick but at a huge cost.

Chapter 12

Full Circle

By the following day, I was back to my normal self, or as normal as I felt it was possible to be now. Some of my friends came around and helped to clear away the mess. We covered up the scrawling on the walls with new posters and prints, anything I could find to hide the messages I had scrawled on the walls. But they were still there, hidden under the pictures of Swiss mountains and Welsh peaks. And I was still angry inside. I knew now that I always would be, but at least I had come to terms with the anger and accepted it. Once again, I would have to find a way to channel it positively in a creative way and not the destructive way in which it had just surfaced. I needed to be strong.

Staffordshire Police were not going to have changed overnight, I knew that. I could not let them get away with treating any other officer in the way they had treated me. I realised that every officer in Staffordshire Police could now know of me and a small minority of them must have been very alarmed. I must not give in. By returning to duty, however difficult that would certainly be, I was proving positively and visibly that I had been right that the way I had been treated was wrong, and that by sticking it out it was possible to win. But in reality, I had lost the spirit to go back; my implicit faith and trust in the police had been shattered.

I tried to ignore my difficulties. A week later I was back on duty, but again I felt physically sick when I approached the station. And there was an uneasy tension in the station; I did not feel comfortable. As quickly as possible I went out on foot patrol around the town centre. Even now, although I was on my own, I was not functioning properly as a police officer. I felt much more vulnerable than I had ever felt on patrol before and then I realised why.

There had always been total faith and trust in colleagues that they would be there for me if I got into difficulties, just as I had done for Colin when he had shouted for help all those months before. But now I did not know how much I could rely on my colleagues to back me up. If I had to call for help, would it come? I didn't know the answer, and that wasn't good enough. As my SDO Rob Rawles had pointed out to me on the night I was suspended, we all work as a team and must trust each other, and he was right. Only it was me who did not trust anyone else now. I booked off duty three hours later. I left the station in a dilemma, I did not ever want to enter it again, but I could not give in.

I put my police duties behind me, I had more important things to work on now. South Staffs Friends were still growing, and it needed increasing amounts of my time. This was the place to put all my energy. But suddenly and without any warning, it all went wrong. At a social meeting soon after Paul took me to one side for a private word. He had heard stories circulating amongst the group about me and they were not very complimentary. Or true. I was shocked. Who would want to say anything like that and why?

We made a few discreet enquiries, and I was even more shocked that the source of the lie was Jeff from the other CAB office and very probably Trevor. What had I done? It became clear they were trying to undermine my authority. What authority though? I didn't have any authority! I was chair of the group simply because I had been instrumental in setting it up and putting most of the work into setting it up. I enjoyed seeing the group grow and helping it to do so. It was a wonderful feeling that we were managing to bring so many people together and to help people, through the switchboard. I never saw myself as having any authority over other members.

The following week the situation worsened, Paul was very off with me, I tried to find out why but all I got was that something had been said, although he would not specify what. I never found out. There was a distinctly bad atmosphere in the group, made worse now by the fact that some members were openly expressing their views that Haz and Joy were not welcome because they were bisexual. I openly supported them, and it made things even worse for me.

I stopped going down to the social meetings and spent my time at the switchboard until one Wednesday evening in mid-December Paul and Gary came down to the CAB having just left the pub. Paul took me to one side to tell me that they had conspired behind my back and had taken and passed a vote of no confidence in me. I was stunned. My problems were starting all over again.

I was so weary of fighting; why should I fight any longer? I was shocked upset and angry all over again. Paul gave me a supportive hug before leaving, but I sensed that he'd had enough of it all. I knew as he left that it might be a long time before I saw him again. It was.

Ironically, the Christmas party was extremely successful, but after Christmas, those people still loyal to me and who still cared about the switchboard and the original aims of South Staffs Friends split away from the social group and continued running the switchboard. We began to meet separately in another pub on the outskirts of the town, but a bitter struggle was developing to get rid of me altogether, I did not understand why until a rumour spread our way a month or so later.

As the AGM approached in late February there were increasingly frantic efforts to get the issue out in the open. Trevor and his gang were equally determined to get rid of me.

We all turned up for the AGM which soon degenerated into a slanging match. I could not believe how evil Trevor and Jeff and one or two of the others could be, how low they could stoop, it easily matched the hatred shown towards me by the police. I made increasingly frantic attempts to sort the situation out, but it became clear that there was nothing I could do, they had made up their minds. I was voted out of South Staffs Friends altogether and effectively banned from the group I had started creating all those months earlier and had put so much of my time and effort into creating. It was so unfair, so wrong. I could not help turning on Trevor as he sat there gloating at his 'victory', I knew what the real reason was, those rumours were probably true. Would he have the nerve to admit it though?

"Is this all because I am a serving *police officer?*" I asked him angrily.

He stared at me icily before replying.

"Yes, that has played a large part in it."

Now I knew, it was true. I stared back at Trevor unable to express the frustration, the anger and the hurt I now felt. I was tired, I'd had enough of the whole bloody affair. How could I ever bridge that gap between those two opposing sides of my life? I remembered that extremely unpleasant meeting in Stoke on Trent all those years earlier when I had been warned not to trust the police. Could I now add to that a distrust of gay society?

I had come full circle.

In the long journey which I had taken since that meeting, a yawning, unbridgeable gulf had emerged. I had tried to cross it but had been pushed into it from opposing sides.

I was determined not to let Trevor and his crowd see how much they had devastated me; I would not give them the satisfaction. I held back the tears. I was sick of fighting now. I got up and walked quietly out of South Staffs Friends for the last time.

Chapter 13

Picking through the Debris

After I was thrown out of South Staffs Friends, I vowed I would never do anything to help gay people again. It was a natural reaction born out of anger and resentment. South Staffs Friends lasted for only a short time after that AGM. I could have drawn some satisfaction from that, and at the time, I did. But tinged with that was regret for what could have been. In the short time it was in existence we helped hundreds of people. If South Staffs Friends had survived, it could still have been helping people today.

I still had a dilemma over what to do about my position with the police. After those two unsatisfactory duties in late 1993, I did not return to duty for several months. I spent a long time thinking about the problem and the issues. I still wanted to continue working as a special constable. And what is more, serving at Rugeley. But it was quite clear that because of the climate that existed at the station it would be exceedingly difficult. It was increasingly obvious that despite my request that Staffordshire Police should deal with the problems raised over my suspension, they never would.

I had pointed out to them just how homophobic the officer in charge of the station was. They *knew* that one of the sergeants had told lies about me. I could have sued the force for libel. That sergeant continued serving at Rugeley, and he left the station eventually as he was promoted to Inspector.

It is surely quite understandable that I would never be received well at Rugeley whilst supervisory and senior officers could get away with their homophobia and bigotry so openly and unchallenged, even perhaps encouraged by the officer in charge. I can illustrate this point by events which have happened since.

I had a chance to meet with Steve Smith one day, long after all the problems had died down to fester beneath the surface again. Steve told me that the reason he had turned his back on me during my suspension was that the other officers at the station were making his life hell simply because he was my friend. He could not cope; he had no choice but to disassociate himself from me. It illustrates the spread and depth of feelings allowed to be expressed at the station during that period. Steve, correctly, realised he had no choice but to do what he did. It would have been a very brave or foolish person to fight it. Steve and I are now friends again, although we rarely socialise together.

I began duties again in the summer of 1994, but the situation was the same; nothing had changed. I still felt physically unwell as I approached the station, and the atmosphere was still tense once inside. I patrolled uneasily, still very unsure of the support I would get if I urgently needed it. I was not happy being on duty at the station.

I carried on but performed fewer duties. After one such duty in 1995, I was approached by one of the other special constables who wanted to speak to me in private. Karen was very unhappy, she wanted to transfer to another station. I asked why and she told me of an incident at the station which she now felt that I ought to know about.

Karen had still been in the station after I had booked off duty sometime earlier when, after I had left, the other officers in the

242

parade room had started to attack me, making homophobic comments. Karen considered they were bad enough to warrant challenging, so she told them it was no way to speak about anyone, let alone a colleague. That was bad enough, it showed that homophobia could still be openly expressed in the station. But what made it worse was what happened next.

Overhearing the exchange, the sergeant in charge of the shift at that time walked through from his office next door and quite openly insulted Karen for supporting me, like *'What the bloody hell are you doing here if you think like that?'* In other words, he felt completely safe in officially supporting the homophobic comments his shift was making. What is more, the sergeant in question is the one who told lies about me in the report to headquarters. I later complained about this officer again but to no effect. Karen applied for and was granted a transfer to Cannock. One officer less at the station would support me now.

It was obvious that blatantly expressed homophobia was allowed to continue at Rugeley, despite my requests that any problems be sorted out. I am sure it is because the officer in charge has never been challenged over his homophobic beliefs and he allowed it to continue unabated in the station.

After Karen told me about that incident I went home and told my partner, John. John then told me of something similar which had happened a few months earlier but had hidden from me until then. I had taken John with me to the station Christmas party at The Horns Pub in December 1994. I did not know what reception we would get but was determined that I was not going to be pushed out. Several specials did speak to us, but the atmosphere was strained, for a large part of the evening we sat on our own. We both later admitted we had felt extremely uncomfortable there.

Whilst there I pointed out the officers to John, including the station inspector. John was buying drinks at the bar shortly after when he heard the inspector, in conversation with another of the officers and they were unaware who was standing next to them; stating his disgust that I was there and that I was a *disgrace to the force.*

I was summoned to a meeting with the new SDO George Graham, and my section officer later in 1995. It was pointed out to me that I had to perform a set number of duties per week, and that I was not doing so, in which case, if I did not start performing regular duties soon, I would have to resign. I pointed out why I was not performing regular duties. I even re-iterated my problems from the period when I was suspended. Both my SDO and section officer feigned surprise at the extent of my problems, they claimed to know nothing about their extent. This was a blatant lie.

I made an appointment to speak to the Divisional Commandant at Cannock, I told him that I wanted the problem to be sorted out properly. We agreed that for a few weeks or months, I would patrol in the company of an officer whom I knew I could trust until I found out where I stood at the station. I was still not convinced that it would work, the real problem was still not being addressed, but I was prepared to go along with it.

In 1995 the chief constable retired, and Mr Giffard took over as chief constable of Staffordshire Police in 1996. I used the opportunity to write to him. In reply, he said: *"I personally have no particular views in this area but it seems to me that returning to what occurred in the main three years ago is rather difficult, especially given that some of the people involved have since retired from the service."*

That proved that even then, the issues were not dealt with

properly.

I had a meeting with the new civilian equal opportunities officer and together we discussed ways forward. We both agreed that the problem at Rugeley needed addressing. It was clear that, at the very least, there was a mutual distrust on both sides. The reason for me was obvious. The problem for other officers is probably because even those officers, if any, who might support me, would feel that because of the stand that I had taken, they were *treading on eggshells*, not knowing what the right thing was to say to me, or how best to treat me, frightened to support me.

I suggested yet again, as a possible way forward, that an open, informal meeting be arranged somehow, between officers from the station and myself, and I emphasised that I would be prepared to talk and bring these problems out in the open, to answer any questions, discuss them, so that we all knew where the 'other side' stood. Another side. It shows just how much of a gulf there was between me and my former colleagues.

I wrote again to Mr Giffard, this time with a detailed outline of everything which had happened to me. His response was the nearest I ever got to an apology from the force, yet still isn't one:

"...I acknowledge that the treatment you received was not in the manner which I would have liked. I do not feel, however, that there would be any benefit to either you or the Force in investigating these issues now."

He went on to express his commitment to the equal opportunities policy and the elimination of discrimination on any grounds in the Force.

When I again contacted the equal opportunities officer, I was told that my suggestion to break the deadlock had been rejected outright. Instead, just a suggestion to contact the divisional chief inspector to organise a return to duties.

Soon after that, I had a meeting with the chief inspector to discuss how I could safely return, and it was suggested that a solution would be to return to duties at the station and work in the enquiry office for a while. It went some way towards addressing the problem but still had not addressed the real issue. The good point about the suggestion was that it would at least allow me to work around and with all the other officers in the station without my worries about patrolling. I would at least be able to find out where I might have problems before resuming normal patrols. But, when I tried to arrange these duties through my SDO he eventually got back to me to tell me that he was having difficulties fitting me into the enquiry office, instead, he would arrange enquiry office duties at Cannock. I refused.

In effect, I was being transferred to another station through the back door. Why were there problems fitting me into work just three or four hours a week helping in the enquiry office at Rugeley? Such duties were never, ever a problem. It was just another excuse to make it difficult for me. It was blindingly clear that the *real* problem had never been addressed.

I was offered, towards the end of my suspension in 1993, the opportunity to lodge an official complaint. I declined to do so then because I did not believe it would ever be dealt with fairly. I am still of the same opinion; at that time, it never could have been dealt with fairly. Staffordshire Police never did deal with the problems I had as an openly gay police officer in their force. There was, however, an achievement which made all those awful few months when I was fighting to remain as a serving gay police officer – all the stress, the destruction, the heartbreak – all worthwhile.

I had a call from Rob Williams, the force welfare officer, quite unexpectedly. He told me that sexual orientation had now

246

been written into the force equal opportunities statement; he also said that I was deeply instrumental in helping to achieve that. That was an achievement at least, for me. It meant that no other officer in Staffordshire Police could so openly be discriminated against for being gay ever again. And it was what started Staffordshire Police on their journey, without me, towards achieving the top position of the Stonewall Workplace Equality Index of the most gay-friendly employers in 2006 under their then Chief Constable John Giffard. For a police force to receive that accolade just nine years after I left was an extraordinary turnaround after everything they had put me through, and it is to the credit of Staffordshire Police that they achieved this.

I went on duty in 1996. It was my last duty. Knowing that nothing had been done to help resolve the problems at the station, I did not return; I had won the battle for sure, but there was still a long way to go, and it wasn't for me; I was exhausted.

I turned my back on the so-called gay community and I turned away from the police. I was determined not to let the anger out in a destructive way ever again. I had to find a way to deal with my anger positively. That's why you're now reading this.

Chapter 14

Closure

My life moved in a quite different direction after I left Staffordshire Police; it had already started before I left. In 1994 I met John. We fell in love and John moved in to live with me at home with my parents and my nan; he was accepted as a new addition to the family by the whole family, and we were together for five years – and we are still the closest of friends to this day, we always will be. It was John who helped me to move on and find another career.

Through John, I applied to and was accepted for a media training course, and qualified in research and journalism, working for the BBC in Birmingham for several happy years. Working at the BBC was such a huge change from working within the police service. My sexuality really didn't matter in the slightest and I was completely open about it from day one.

I left the BBC in 2002 when I was made redundant as the BBC moved to the Mailbox from Pebble Mill. I turned towards graphic design again, this time all created on the computer. I lost my father in 2002 and my mother in 2013 after which I moved to Lichfield, eight miles from Rugeley, living within the beautiful Cathedral Close. I now work at the Cathedral School where I am a matron to the choristers, and I love my job and the place I work.

The Covid-19 Pandemic which led to the national lockdown in the Spring of 2020, left lots of free time for many, including me, to find things to do, and I re-visited this manuscript. Re-visiting the manuscript after twenty-seven years was an interesting and cathartic experience. It all seemed so raw, so immediate once again and extremely challenging to read in places, but the passage of time had put a slightly different perspective on it for me. I talked to lots of friends and colleagues about it and it was suggested by several of them that I should look at getting it published. Something was holding me back though and I couldn't work out what it was.

In the summer of 2022, I became ill. My colleagues had noticed me going downhill months before I became aware of it. I started getting flashbacks of the assault in 1993 which could have so easily killed me. I realised I'd had one whilst at the caravan with Paul in 1993 but didn't understand it then. But this time the flashbacks became relentless; most of my waking day my brain was taking me straight back to the kicking in the patrol car and all the events over the following months which had traumatised me. Every time I relaxed or went to sleep, I was woken up by punching the back of the bed or sofa, trying to stop the assailant from kicking me. I was diagnosed with severe, delayed PTSD and at once I was put on a course of CBT therapy. This all started within three days of going to my surgery and asking for help. Thank you, NHS.

What became clear was that in 1993 I didn't get any support for PTSD which began shortly after the assault. It was hardly known about then. It's why I became depressed and why my anxiety increased so much that I got upset with Paul, which led to my suspension on sick leave.

What also became clear was that there had never been any closure to the horrific events of 1993. There was never any resolution, no acceptance of wrongdoing, no apology.

The CBT therapy was intense but successful in 'putting to bed' the assault, putting it into deep memory. I realised though that I needed to get closure for the period when Staffordshire Police tried to get rid of me for being a gay police officer in the months which followed the assault. I wrote to them.

In the late Autumn of 2022, I had a meeting at Staffordshire Police Headquarters. This was a meeting I had requested. Staffordshire Police had moved their headquarters to another complex on the other side of Stafford, so I had no qualms about going there to meet them. I knew that the force was now a quite different place to work than it had been in 1993.

It was a momentous event for me. I had a very productive meeting with a sergeant from the Professional Standards Department, and also present was a serving gay officer. I was asked to tell them exactly what had happened almost thirty years before. They were both shocked and horrified when I talked through the events recounted in this narrative.

I was given a formal, and sincere, apology for the way the force had treated me in 1993 and afterwards.

The serving gay police officer who works in the LGBTQ+ department gave me a heartfelt and very genuine thank you from himself and on behalf of all the other serving officers who were LGBTQ+ within Staffordshire Police since 1993, when sexuality was added to the Equal Opportunities Policy, for kick-starting the change which led to the force making it much easier for them to serve. This thank you, more than anything else, was the real closure I had so desperately needed.

I stressed right at the start of the meeting that I didn't want the meeting to be one-sided. I wanted it to be a positive meeting for both sides, somehow. I didn't have an axe to grind, Staffordshire Police was not the enemy. I certainly needed closure, and I got it. That was the positive outcome I needed. In the end, it was more than I could have ever hoped for.

I was offered a place as a member of the Staffordshire Police Independent Advisory Group, and I accepted the offer. IAGs were set up in all forces as a recommendation of the Stephen Lawrence Inquiry. It was suggested that I had a unique and valuable experience to offer Staffordshire Police. I am really excited to open a new chapter with Staffordshire Police, to be able to contribute my experiences positively for the force and to help them move forward smoothly with other issues too.

A week or two after my meeting at headquarters and as my CBT was nearing closure, a strange thing happened. I felt odd; much different to how I would usually feel. I couldn't explain it at all, but the feeling grew, and it wasn't anything worrying or bad. It was all very strange! At my penultimate CBT session with my therapist, we worked it out. I realised that finally, at last, after almost thirty years of carrying it; the trauma and the baggage from those months fighting Staffordshire Police…is gone. Completely gone! Dealt with! I haven't felt like this for more than thirty years! I couldn't quite believe it!

There is one other factor about my time as a serving police officer which has become known since leaving Staffordshire Police, and which I think is interesting. I am now diagnosed with ASD – Autistic Spectrum Disorder. As my consultant who diagnosed me told me, this part of the ASD spectrum used to be known as Aspergers. I don't see my ASD as a disability but as a *different* ability. Certainly, there are some negative traits because of it, but there are also many positive traits.

My brain sees things very clearly in black and white, right or wrong, with no grey areas. That made learning and understanding criminal law quite easy. So easy that it gave me time to think about how to deal with incidents; how much and which side of the law an incident fell.

Another autistic trait I have is being mute when I face aggression or anger. My brain cannot process how to deal with aggression, so I become mute, unable to say anything at all. Usually, I also don't have any emotions at that time. So, when we are ordered to remain calm and not to make any arrests as public disorder events build up, when a very drunk youth stands in front of me, spitting at me (which is an assault), trying to wind me up, or trying to frighten me – no feelings, nothing! Just blank. No high emotion of any sort. I might carry on thinking about what the right thing is to do, or I might wonder what I might have for dinner tonight. It is a good trait, but there was one incident where this trait worked against me.

If I had been able to shout to the driver when I was being kicked half to death, it might have been stopped much earlier. But I was mute. Unable to shout out that I needed help!

There is another good autistic trait which helped me so much in 1993. If you know anyone who is on the autistic spectrum, that when they know that an issue is wrong, it is always challenged and it is impossible to stand down, to give in. Utterly impossible. Staffordshire Police didn't realise that when I refused to be removed because I'm gay. Neither did I then; I didn't know what it meant to be autistic. I wasn't diagnosed until many years later, but I did know that I absolutely couldn't let Staffordshire Police get away with what they were trying to do.

Finally, there is one very unlikely person who I need to thank. Since quite young I was slightly short-sighted. When I joined the police service, I quickly found out that wearing glasses was dangerous for the glasses. One evening, helping a colleague arrest a youth who climbed over a wall and was about to break into a shop, three of us went to help arrest him. I was the first over the wall and helped him to arrest the youth while the other two officers were climbing over.

We were tussling on the ground to get handcuffs on the offender and my glasses were knocked off and flew across the tarmac. All I could see were two large sets of boots trying to get near us to help. My glasses! Mind my bloody glasses! Don't trample on them, please! Fortunately, a PC attached to one of the sets of boots picked my glasses up for me and kept them safe. Phew! Oh, and then we got the handcuffs on the youth. And my glasses were safe. Within a month, I was wearing contact lenses. Much safer!

A few years later, after I had left the police service, I was shocked to find out from my optician that I had cataracts in both eyes. I was only in my thirties! They were traumatic cataracts caused by the assault in 1993.

And so, several years further on, I had the damaged, cloudy, traumatised lenses in both eyes, replaced by artificial ones which instantly gave me clear, perfect vision again, but more importantly, corrected my shortsight – I no longer needed glasses or contact lenses! Thank you, whoever you are!

Post Script

Right at the start of this narrative I encountered extreme distrust of Staffordshire Police from the gay community. I fled from that then because I was just starting my training within Staffordshire Police and I couldn't reconcile the two.

Having fought and won my case as a serving gay officer within Staffordshire Police, where this distrust of the police in Staffordshire was verified, and subsequently thrown out of the gay helpline and support group which I'd set up because of my role as a Police officer, those two aspects of my life seemed utterly unbridgeable then. I walked away from both.

When I originally wrote this narrative almost thirty years ago I had no desire to have it published. It was written as a cathartic exercise to help me deal with what had just happened. I didn't see it as publishable, but also, dramatically, it didn't have the closure it needed.

At no time did I ever fall out with Staffordshire Police. My argument was not with the organisation, but with specific people within it. I was and always have been proud to serve in Staffordshire Police. Therefore, I could never consider this story to be made public until I had the positive closure I got in 2022. I'm still immensely proud to have served as an officer in the force and again now as a member of the IAG.

The closure of these issues, when Staffordshire Police formally apologised to me in late 2022 for the way I had been treated, and also thanked by a serving gay police officer for starting off the change in attitude, was the start of the closure which I desperately needed. But even that wasn't complete closure.

In July 2023, I went with friends to Lichfield Pride, something I never thought I would do again, even just a year ago. It was a joyous two days, if a little damp the first day. My friend Stevie is Equalities Officer for the NEU in Staffordshire so I spent time at the NEU stand with him and Bob, his husband. The stand next door was Staffordshire Police. I happily spent time chatting with some of the gay officers there, some even wearing rainbow-striped epaulettes for the day. I may even be helping Staffordshire Police at the next local Pride Day in a few weeks. The gay community and the police were poles apart thirty years ago in Staffordshire; I had found myself attacked from both sides.

Finally, that seemingly unbridgeable gulf in my life has been bridged. I now feel that I've found the closure I needed. I'm gay! I'm happy! Overjoyed that this story is now finally complete. This really is the end of that chapter of my life. I can now start looking ahead to a future where I'm gay and working for Staffordshire Police and it really doesn't matter. The schism in my life is closed. Thanks for reading!